William Young

The Spirit of Athens

Being a Political and Philosophical Investigation of the History of that Republic

William Young

The Spirit of Athens
Being a Political and Philosophical Investigation of the History of that Republic

ISBN/EAN: 9783337078010

Printed in Europe, USA, Canada, Australia, Japan

Cover: Foto ©ninafisch / pixelio.de

More available books at **www.hansebooks.com**

THE
SPIRIT of ATHENS.

BEING

A POLITICAL and PHILOSOPHICAL

INVESTIGATION

OF THE

HISTORY of that REPUBLIC.

By WILLIAM YOUNG, Esq;

Πασα πολιτεια ΨΥΧΗ της πολεως εστι, τοσαυτην εχυσα δυναμιν ωσπερ εν σωματι φρονησις.   Isocrat. in Panath.

LONDON:
Printed for J. ROBSON, New Bond Street.

MDCCLXXVII.

PREFACE.

—M*ULTUM legendum esse, non multa,*——is an adage of antiquity replete with a deep and excellent sense;—it means that much reading implies not much knowledge, and that study leadeth not necessarily to wisdom;—it teaches that to profit of our application, whilst we peruse one book, we should think another; and instead of being *librorum helluones* give the mind exercise and time wherewith to digest a moderate and wholesome fare;—it inculcates, that to run over many authors, may to the language of pedantry gain the title of learning; but that attentively to penetrate the sense of a few, is the way to science.

All men however have not equal acuteness to develope, equal assiduity to pursue, or equal memory to retain the subject-matter of a book: says Montaigne—" I have read an hundred things in Titus Livius, that have escaped the observations of others, and Plutarch has read an hundred more there, besides what I was able to discover;"—so far I agree with this sensible essayist; but when he adds,—" and more perhaps than Livy ever *inserted* in his book,—either I do not understand, or I must oppose, or must refine upon, the sense of the text; for though an antiquary or chronologist may take advantage of some trivial circumstance to falsely presume the authenticity of an epoch or of a relict, yet to him who reads history, not as the history of dates and pagods, but of men, it hath recondite in it all the lessons of ethics and policy that he can make himself master of from the perusal: every annalist must be under the predicament of teaching more than himself knows to those who come after him, and

who

who of courſe connecting his particular link of the chain as well with the ſucceeding as with the foregoing ſeries, may deduce what the author could never ſurmiſe to have been in his work;—a ruſtic makes a lever to riſe, another employs it to aſcertain the weight, nor is this uſe the leſs inherent in the inſtrument for the ignorance of its firſt artificer: ſo far I premiſe to obviate the objections I forſee may be made to this treatiſe, as too fancyfully inveſtigating the ſubject, and extracting often from the text philoſophy and politics when no ſuch deductions ſhould be made, and no ſuch leſſons (to uſe a word of Montaigne's tranſlator) were ever *inſerted* in my originals.

Ariſtotle in his ninth chapter of poetics, diſcriminating hiſtory from poetry, makes not the difference to conſiſt in the meaſure and harmony of verſe,—" the hiſtories
" of Herodotus (ſays he) though put into
" metre, would not conſtitute a poem;
" hiſtory teaches what has been, poetry
" what

"what may be; wherefore, poetry is of a more *philosophical* and *didactic** spirit than history;——this treating of things generally, the latter individually." This opinion of Aristotle that the epic muse was a better and more comprehensive teacher than the historic, first gave me the idea of writing the following work; I could not but imagine that this deep-thinking man had once in his life decided too lightly:— that the poet might in an Æneas combine the mental qualities of many, as well as the painter draw the various beauties of nature into one piece of art, I could well conceive;—and that history, when it delineated an individual, was confined to a narrower compass, than the canvass spread to the lavish hand of fancy, I could not

but

---

* The word σπουδαιότερον in the version is rendered by *res magis seria;* in this sense given us by the Latin translator (if any sense) I have not taken it. σπυδαιος ο αξιος σπυδης——deserving study——informative to the student— didactic. Scapula v. deriv. verb. σπυδω.

but allow; but hiftory (thought I) is not the memoirs of one man, but the hiftory of men; it is perverted when employed in the fervice of Cæfar; and not of Rome; national characteriftic, as much or more than private character, fhould be obvioufly deducible from this fort of work; and if thus treated (and thus it fhould be treatted) furely hiftory may teem with as much philofophic theory as poetry: in the annals of an united people we find matter for general pofitions, and the particular examples interfperfed affift us in the analyfis or compofition of our fyftem;——they form a fet of rudiments to the σύνταξις, which poetry can never have fo compleat; for many an incident replete with influence may not fuit its dignity, and the mention of many a pregnant circumftance may be exploded, as not being coincident with the rules of the art,—*primo afpectu levia* (fays Tacitus) *ex queis magnarum fæpe rerum motus oriuntur:* poetry indeed (as obferves the ftagyrite)

gyrite) tells us what may be; but as a tutoress of morals and of wisdom, she can only tell what may be, by collecting, combining, and modifying what has been; and this (as the following essay may serve to elucidate) is equally the province of history: poetry may, perhaps, show the scene to a dim eye, in larger quarries, and in stronger colours; to gain this advantage, likewise over to history, and to paint a forcible and expressive picture of my subject, I have changed the attitudes of some figures, I have transposed others, and approximated them to a stronger contrast, or to a more glaring light; many are the anachronisms which this free, or rather libertine, mode of writing has betrayed me into;—but the consequence was unavoidable, and I hope this confession, as it cautions the unlearned against error, may serve to obviate the strictures of the critical. My design is from the annals of men and things to extract the spirit of character and event, with the narrative to interweave the moral, and to give

at

at once the hiftory and its comment; and in this, my book may be of fome ufe to the young, or to the fuperficial ftudent;— it may teach him that the ancient Greek hiftory is fraught with fomething more than apothegm and anecdote,—— that to know the names of Marathon and Salamis, of Codrus, or of Cimon, (to purfue a metaphor of Mr. Burke's) is merely to know the *land-marks* of hiftory, and not the country,—that to a fagacious traveller the country is the object,——its abrupt breaks, its gentler declivities, its culture, and its produce: he muft not expect to meet with his acquaintance from the Pantheon; —the heroes of fable have found no admittance in this work;——well were it, if no-nothing of more importance to the hiftory was omitted!—In my courfe many a flower have I difregarded, that others have ftayed to pluck, and perchance, fometimes a fimple have I culled, which another hath neglected; what I have idly rejected, and what, perhaps, as idly chofen, may equally

fubject

subject me to censure;——I humbly submit to it, nor will I prolong this preface to deprecate its severity,——nor, in the language of deference, to hint pretensions, nor to jingle a quaint antithesis to public amusement, and to public utility;--to say I wrote for either, were vain as it is false;——I wrote the following book to beguile an idle time, and I know no better reason for publishing, than because——I have wrote, it.

CONTENTS.

CONTENTS.

BOOK THE FIRST.

CHAP. I.
Introductory.—On Ancient History.   Page 1

CHAP. II.
Of the Population of Attica.—Of the Progress of Society.   11

CHAP. III.
Of the Colonies acceding to the original Settlement.—Of the Advantages thence accruing to the Community.—Of the Heroic Age.   20

CHAP. IV.
Of the Kings, and of the first Archons of Athens.   28

Chap. V.
Of the Legiflation of Solon. —— 33

Chap. VI.
Of Pififtratus. —— —— 44

Chap. VII.
Of Hipparchus.—Of Ariftogeiton and Harmodius.—Of the Lover and beloved. 49

Chap. VIII.
Of the Final expulfion of the Pififtratide.—Of a Democracy.—Of the Oftracifm. 56

Chap. IX.
Of Governments.—Of the energy of a newly formed Republic.—Of the Progrefs of Athens —— —— 69

Chap. X.
Of Liberty.—Of Colonies.—Of the further Progrefs of Athens. —— 76

Chap. XI.
Of the firft Perfian war.—Condemnation of Miltiades.—Further thoughts concerning the Oftracifm. —— 84

CONTENTS.

Chap. XII.
Of the second Persian War.   97

Chap. XIII.
Of Great Men.—Athens rebuilt.—Consequences of the Persian War.—Supremacy of Athens.   115

✳✳✳✳✳✳✳✳✳✳✳✳✳✳✳✳✳✳✳✳✳✳✳✳

BOOK THE SECOND.

Chap. I.
OF the principles of happiness national and private.—Of Conquest—Of the acquisitions and power of Athens.   Page 131

Chap. II.
Of Arts.   145

Chap. III.
Of Manners.   160

Chap. IV.
Of Pericles.—Of the Dominion of Athens.—Of the Peloponnesian War to the Argive alliance. — 169

Chap. V.
Of Navigation and Commerce.—Of the Sicilian Expedition. — 190

Chap. VI.
Continuation of the Peloponnesian war.--Revolutions at Athens.—Conclusion of the War, subversion of the Commonwealth and establishment of the Oligarchy. 202

Chap. VII.
Of the Expedition of the Ten Thousand.—Parallel of the Commentaries of Xenophon and of Cæsar. — 215

Chap. VIII.
Of Socrates. — 233

Chap. IX.
Restoration of the Commonwealth. 240

Chap. X.
Of the degradation of the republic in its
contests

CONTENTS.

contests with Philip.——Temper of the Times, deduced from the Orations of Demosthenes. —— 253

CHAP. XI.
Of the Holy War. —— 277

CHAP. XII.
From the Battle of Chæronea to the surrender of the Commonwealth to Antipater, and the extinction of the SPIRIT OF ATHENS. ——— 288

ERRATA.

Page. Line.
6— 4. *For* undetermined *read* undermined
21—11. ——— for ——— far
38—10. ——— gone the ——— gone through the
42— 3. ——— jataque ——— juraque
67—13. ——— But it is not ——— But is not
235— 9. ——— insertion ——— assertion
244— 3. ——— the ——— this
261—13. ——— Pagazæ ——— Pagasæ

THE
SPIRIT OF ATHENS.

BOOK THE FIRST.

CHAP. I.

THE wildeſt narratives of remote antiquity, however little to be depended on for veracity, are not wholly to be regarded as the ſports of roving fantaſtic genius, or as uſeful, merely as fables bearing a deep and beautiful moral: they are ſtill more ſtriking as types of the ſpirit and purſuits of the age they relate to. The mind of man untutored in philoſophical truths recurs naturally to the marvellous; blind to the inherent wonders of every the minuteſt part of the creation, he himſelf imagines new miracles for the deity of his

his foul;—each god, each demigod, each hero, is thus aggrandized by the fertile enthusiasm of his adherents, who unwilling to allow the confessed superiority to a being noways essentially differing from themselves, invest him with such powers, and attribute to him such actions, as their wanton zeal may suggest, or wild credulity patronize.—Still however, the virtues held up to admiration, are the virtues of the age that admires: the prejudices and pursuits of the fabulist enter into the delineation of the creature of his fancy, however perfect he may design him, and as our poet or other writer is a member of, and writes but for his community, we may pronounce that his embellishments, though but an airy superstructure, are yet raised on a known and good foundation, and that his recital is at least consonant to the amusement and taste of his cotemporaries.

' Thus the memoirs of chivalry or stories of more ancient heroism inform, as well as delight; the age of gallant knighthood is perhaps better described, in Amadis, than by Mezeray; Woden and his followers are better known from a runic song, than from a monkish historian; and in the tales of Hercules and the Argonauts, the spirit of those remote times is better traced than it could be in the book of any strict conformer to truth and fact: we thus get acquainted with the prior ages by fables, as with succeeding from records, nor is the study thereof to be slighted, as long as the improveability of man is thought worthy to hold a place in his speculations; and the progress and various steps and changes of the human mind are deemed proper objects of its enquiry. In such philosophical pursuit the reading of fabulous history has its peculiar use, but further is not to be expected from it; the infancy of human nature can no more serve as example to man in an improved state, than the child's whims to one in years, in whose deeper thoughts and studies they may yet profitably find a place.

By many, and indeed most of the learned, it hath been deemed difficult to draw the line in ancient history between the fabulous and the authentic; but here the word fabulous bears another sense, and the opposition of terms may simply be construed into *true* and *false*: The ten first books of Livy have been stigmatized with the term *fabulous*,—meaning solely that the facts therein represented are singular, doubtful, and in many cases stated as such, by the very author; but yet are they not to be classed with the tales of

poetry

poetry:—their leſſon is deep and they bear a ſtrong and pointed character,——whether after the life or not, the picture hath a phyſiognomy moſt intereſting, and ſo well elucidated by the maſterly touches of the painter, that equal profit and pleaſure reſult from the niceſt conſideration of it. It is enough that the politic Machiavel hath dedicated the moſt ſterling labours of his pen to reflections on this theme; Let the antiquary bring his medals, or the book-learned his books to the controverſy—the pedant would cleanſe the root and filth is his portion, whilſt the florentine bee pitched on the lively flower is ſucking the ſweeteſt honey from each petal! Little doth it matter I think where the record is of ſo old a date, and affects not any right or property, and gives no authority to any ſyſtem, and brings no weight of favor or oppoſition to the opinions of the day;—little doth it matter, whether the hiſtory is compoſed of abſolute facts, ſo long as it bears the characteriſtics of truth and nature.—The Venus of Zeuxis ſurely might be pronounced equally eſtimable, whether the ſtory of the five beauties of Agrigentum was true or falſe.

Lord Bolingbroke looking over the general proſpect of hiſtory ancient, and modern, and

con-

considering its tendency merely as to the knowledge of men and manners, says—he would chearfully exchange the books of Livy we have, for those we have not; he enumerates the advantages Livy had in his latter books of painting characters he knew, and those too of the greatest; of describing events he was concerned in, facts he had from the immediate actors,— quæque ipse miserrima vidit.

But surely a cotemporary historian of such turbulent times might be too apt to exagerate through adulation or conceal through fear; to give the precepts not of the philosopher, but partizan; and colour facts into harmony with his own system of patriotism or friendship. Cæcina in his letter to Cicero says *—" much have " I been necessitated to refrain, many things have " I been obliged to pass over lightly, many to " curtail, and very many absolutely to omit— " thus circumscrib'd restricted and broken as it " is, what pleasure or what useful information " can be expected from the recital?" So wrote the historian Cæcina, and so probably did Livy write; but this apart;—have we not sufficient

pages

* —Sed tamen me sustinui, multa minui, multa sustuli, complura ne posui quidem;—sic tot malis cum vinctum tum fractum studium scribendi, quid dignum auribus, aut probabile potest afferri? Ciceron. Ep. fam. Lib. 6. Epist. 7.

pages blotted with the follies and vices of great men? Have we no annals to refer to for the consequences of luxury, the progress of venality and corruption, and liberty undetermined? Or are we yet to learn that one and the same is the downfall of virtue and of freedom, and that with equal pace individuals become vicious, and a community enslaved? Writings enough exist tracing the corruption of men and states through every mode and degree;—the period of antiquity characterised by a wild and impetuous generosity, by an enthusiastic patriotism and daring love of freedom,——that age wherein the virtues were indebted to the passions for more, than ever since the boasted aid of reason could afford them, has been delineated but by few great masters; and for the honour of humanity not a line thereof should be effaced. I would not barter one page of the early accounts of the republics of Athens or of Rome for the most accurate acquaintance with all that Augustus ever did or thought.

Surely in every mind there is an emulation of virtuous superiority, which, however fortune or the meaner passions may hebetate its powers, still at every example of success in the particular objects of its predilection, glows into a momentary flame, which from frequent resuscitation may

acquire

acquire a stability and strength sufficient to reach at the attainment of, what, at first was regarded solely as matter of admiration: the idea of imitation which hath thus enraptured the fancy, may in times of perilous crisis somewhat elevate the mind, and influence the conduct; and if such ever may be the effect, what other lecture can balance the utility of that, which thus animates the man and urges him to noble and disinterested services in a good, great, and public cause.

The history of intellect may be typified by the Ægyptian Nile which long pours on and hurries all away in one collected channel; as it advances it divides into various branches and at length breaks in many and widely distant streams towards the great gulph, into which according to their respective forces, they for a time continue their way, till finally all are lost and confused in the abyss: in the age of golden simplicity and ignorance the objects and pursuits of mankind were but little varied, their thoughts were confined to their common wants, their passions mostly concentered in some common local prejudice or affection; as the genius became elevated, and the judgment tutored by successive experience, and the influence of general acquisitions fitions of arts and of knowledge, the human mind proved its sureſt diſtinction from inſtinct by the *varieties* of its tendency, its force, and its concluſions, in its progreſs to the ſuperior objects' of reaſon, the great truths, *natural, moral,* and *political,*—at length refined and puſhed to the extremity each reſearch cloſes in error and in darkneſs.

In this hiſtory of intellect and manners there was an epoch when men had characters happily combining the uniform and various—viewing that period of antiquity we ſeem to deſcry a landſcape of a bold and maſſive taſte of compoſition, contraſted with ſtrong light and ſhade, and of a brilliant touch of colour, and much harmony; whilſt in the modern age we behold a ſcene flittered into a multiplicity of luminous ſpots, and gaudy without effect;—perhaps it is too near the eye;—perhaps it may be ſaid that the favorite ſcene of ancient hiſtory merely appears the more beautiful, as a picture mellowed by age,—as a rude but diſtant proſpect harmonized by the intervening medium, and loſing all its abrupt breaks and deformities in the diſtance; whilſt modern hiſtory, (as it were) a foreground, appears ſpotted with weeds and reptiles which belong equally to the further

ſcene

scene but are there less conspicuous to the eye:—but surely in the old times I would allude to, there was something essentially distinguishing the characters of mankind, and absolutely giving them a form and complexion differing from those of to-day.

Men when first called from the mere society of family and propinquity to more extensive duties, and a new sort of combination, were fond of the novelty, and the compact was looked up to by every eye: *then*, individuals formed a community;—*now*, more properly a community may be said to be of individuals;—*then*, the interest of the whole was that of each;—*now*, the inverse is adopted, and each would operate on the whole. The genius of patriotism which animated every breast no longer exists;—we wonder at its effects;—we doubt that the Greek Codrus or Roman Decii devoted themselves;—and that the elder Brutus should sacrifice the dearest tyes of nature to a sentiment we so little know the force of, now seems singular if not impossible: and yet Galileo cried—" *et tamen movet,*" and would have died for a mere system; and millions of religious zealots have daringly perished in defence of opinions themselves understood not; and shall we pay so little respect to

mankind

mankind as to suppose them capable of such efforts in favor of vanity or of ignorance, and not equally brave in support of the liberal and benevolent sentiments, the social and spirited principles, on which those fam'd establishments were secured, their united labors had formed, their reason approved, and their habits and their happiness required!

At least condemn them not unheard; listen once more to a testimony in their favor; attend to the history of Athens.

CHAP.

CHAP. II.

GREECE was situated under a benign latitude, and whilst its inhabitants were but few, its spontaneous fertility easily satisfied its pastoral possessors, who with their herds rov'd peaceably from spot to spot, as its beauties or conveniences invited; and left it, as satiety or its harrassed soil urged to a new situation.

Under such circumstances of peace and secured felicity, no wonder that population encreased; and the bands of propinquity then from their too great extent being rent and broken, the detached parties became more in number, and the face of the country gradually was covered with a diversity of people, who retained but little sense of common family, and much of private interest.

The wandering herd often now found the richest pasturage preoccupied, and a system of such appropriation being little understood by savages, who heretofore deemed the earth, as heavens, common to all; a claim to participate brought on contention, and the victorious took

possession

poffeffion of the lands till fuch time as other intruders with better pretenfions of ftrength expelled the conquerors, and fucceeded to an
equally hoftile and precarious fettlement.

The tribes broken, feparated, and defpoiled
of their flocks, fled to the mountains; till em-
boldened by hunger and urged by revenge, they
ventured from their lurking places in fmall but
defperate bands, to procure a fuftenance and fa-
tiate their rage by depredations on their former
invaders. The fhepherds foon learnt to dread,
and to defend themfelves againft, thefe new enemies: fmall bodies ftrengthened themfelves by
coalition, and all parties feemed ftudious of the
means to repel, or to annoy an enemy: arms
were in every hand; habit enured to danger;
and the glory of conqueft too began to enforce
its plea.

The moft verdant mead, the moft flourifhing
grove, the fweeteft fpring fucceffively bleft the
ftrongeft; and all the goods man could then
know, depended on his courage to attempt, or
prowefs to maintain them. The richeft plains
of Greece were fcenes of continual war; and all
the evils, which the untutor'd barbarity of fa-
vages ordinarily annexes to conqueft, conjoined
to make the weaker for ever forego that bounty

of

of Nature, they could enjoy but for so little a time, and with so much danger: other fields were they to seek whose poverty might ensure them from desolation, and rude and rocky surface might yet afford a cave hospitable to the wretched;—a possession unmolested as unenvied by their more potent neighbours.

Attica, a large tract of country poor of those natural advantages which were, and might again be the subject of contention, seemed a proper place of settlement for these wanderers;—thus as Rome owed its population to crimes, so did Athens to misery; and by a singular fatality the two most virtuous and most powerful republics of the ancient world, were founded by the wicked, and by the weak!

No longer could the people subsist from the spontaneous bounties of the earth; nature was to be courted for sustenance; the golden age of indolence was past, and man was to live but by the sweat of his brow. Every one equally subsisting from toil, industry soon put in a new and allowed claim to property; he that had sown the grain reaped the harvest, and prescription gradually cemented this corner stone of political institution. If it was not a settled state, it was a fraternity directed by known and
fixed

fixed regulations; and its union and progreſſive arts gave them an evident ſuperiority over the brutal ſtrength of any who might dare to attack them in their place of retreat, and ravage the fields endeared by their labours.

As ſelf-love is the parent of ſocial, ſo are private affections of public; attachment, as it were, from our little home in the center eradiates to the very periphery, and comprehends the great circle of the common-wealth. Herein behold the ground-work of patriotiſm! Faſtened by the habits of peace and competence to the ſame grounds when old which their infancy ſported in, reciprocal obligation had time to take root, and the fruits were a grateful and diffuſive benevolence; the intereſt, not of families only, but of men, ſeemed united, and whoever ſhould attempt to ſever thoſe bands, was by all conſidered as having no claim to that ſociety he inſulted. Peace was to all but to him who invaded it!

It is in the barren ſoil that genius and induſtry take the earlieſt root; the ſterility of nature proves a ſpur to art, and invention is awakened by the clamours of neceſſity: ſoon the human mind is indebted to its activity for ſtill further force, and purſuing the paths which want or appetite

petite point to, is captivated with the prospects opening on either side, and at length boldly deviates into the wilds of knowledge and pleasure.

Thus our community quickly outstripped its once more happy and formidable neighbours, in the career of enjoyments and of power, whilst ease and plenty were successively the result of industrious arts, and mental quickness and social combination were more than a match for robust but divided savages.

The rough diamonds from the mine but little vary, it is when polished, that we distinguish the beauties or dullness of the water, the flaw, or pure, or tinted brilliant; so civilization discovers the susceptibility and value of each mind, and in the infancy of policy, where no prescription hath sway, inequality of intellect, gradually produces correspondent degrees of command and subserviency. Aristotle hath set out in his politics with much study and pains, and much speculation on, and many reasonings for this hypothesis; but surely every ox that draws the plough is sufficient proof of the assertion! from man to man still greater is the subjection whilst admiration locks, or gratitude gilds, the chains himself from conscious inferiority hath imposed.

Mark

Mark the picture of society which now presents itself to view—genius working not on luxuries or refinements, but confined to an investigation of the common arts and neceffaries of life; and weaknefs courting it for a participation of its comforts; and paying the debt of gratitude, or earneft of expectancy, with menial fervice and affiftance.

In an earlier period, the cave was a refuge common to all, the acorn was to be plucked by every hand, and in the calm of univerfal ignorance, knowledge or activity, for the courfe lay dormant; and its claims were not known, not underftood, or not allowed: but now the man of reafon culled new bleffings from the earth, and where nature feemed deficient, found refources of happinefs and eafe in his own inventive faculties; nor is it wonderful, that thofe whofe powers were inadequate to their wants, fhould purchafe fhelter in his hut, warmth from his fire, or fuftenance from his roots, with obfequious attention to ferve and venerate the benefactor: with deference to fome over learned men, who have made of late fo many *important* and *accurate* deductions from mythology, we will venture to fuppofe, that *whoever* firft planted a twig, or fowed a grain, or ftruck fire

from

from a flint, thence forward, became a character divine; and that *every spot* had its race of deities—its Bacchus, its Ceres, and its Vulcan.

The advantages accruing from this union of the wife and strong, were too obvious to ceafe with the first projector; his name was reverenced and invoked by his adherents, and his temporal power and rule were delegated to the man, whom superior acutenefs diftinguifhed, or prefumption introduced; the latter in the first inftance, fpecioufly cloathed with the fpirit of enterprize, were admitted into competition with the wife and the expert; but as in thofe times the only title to rule, was the conferring of benefits, of which every fubject was individually to partake, and capable too of ftriking the balance between fervices paid, and good received; thefe intruders were fpeedily difgraced, and perhaps in the fhock of public commotion, were detached from the general body, and with a few others whom fympathy or refentment connected with them, were left to rely on that ftrength which paffion and felf-confidence rendered at once unfit for rule, and impatient of fubjection.

They retired to their old manfions of refuge among the woods and rocks—but the cavern was grown damp and gloomy, and the wind had

learnt

learnt to chill, and the sun to scorch; and past use had taught that these evils might be avoided, and from present inexpertness they knew not how!

As in the progress of the individual from infancy to maturity, so in the history of the species, we find that the passions have born fruit, when the blossoms of reason but peeped from the bud: happily in the first instance the earlier violences of the youth may at once be calmed and tutored, and even their effects medicated by the interposition of those who have at once superior reason to urge, and strength to restrain: but who is to coerce the savage,—whose life fills up an impetuous moment of puberty, in the long progressive history of his kind; who hath awakened at once to wishes and to impotence; to the passions of man, and scarcely to the instinct of the brute! Envy without emulation, gloomy discontent, and the rage of unsated appetites— (the feeble ray of reason directing to the object, without throwing sufficient light to develope its moral and proper use, duties, and consequences;) what a dreadful animal must they form! and such was man, when (in the case above mentioned) he recurred to solitude with the full harvest of wants and passions, he had known, and only known how to reap in the fields of society.

In

In thefe times every diftrict had its Cacus; and as attack neceffarily enforces defence, every tribe its Hercules. In the courfe of a few years, the imitative faculty of man muft have made fuch progrefs, and the connexions within the pale of fociety have become fo much more complicated, and the dangers from without, fo much more frequent and important, that the brave and the judicious might readily be fuppofed to fupercede the pretenfions of the projector or artificer, with whom too fo many now claimed in common. The patriarch ruler gave out fimple laws, or rather maxims to his people, decided between them, repelled their enemies, and facrificed to their gods—he was their judge, their hero and their prieft; he was the only flave in the domain, for the black fpirit of defpotifm was as yet confined within the magic circle of its duties, which when it tranfgreffed, the charm of authority and pre-eminence was inftantaneoufly diffolved.

CHAP.

CHAP. III.

WE have traced the first population of Attica; we have marked the progressive culture of people and of soil; and from a mere society of nature, seen men gradually accumulate on the experience of their forefathers, and lay the ground-work of art and of policy, of the comforts of life and of the means to ensure them: but the establishment had now attained that point in progress, that no longer urged by the same necessities, it was not to be expected they should continue the same speed in the career of improvement: Society was now in some measure formed and regulated, and each individual born to some fixed relation in it, cramped by the pursuits and authority of a parent, and restrained by the peace and love of order that prevailed throughout, could no longer innovate with applause or even safety: The short season of autumn may suffice for the vintage, but whole years are required to mellow and perfect the production! if some extraordinary casualty

happened

happened not, the future progress of this people was to be the flow and imperceptible work of ages;—happily such casualty was not wanting.

It must be allowed that soil and climate operate much on the constitution and temperament of the body, and the subtlety of the nervous fluid, the crassitude of the blood, the relaxation or tension of muscle, (in a word) the texture of the whole frame being thus dependant on, and varying with exterior causes; for as their influence acts, the whole animal man must differ in his strength, passions or acuteness, and be accordingly fit or unfit for diverse pursuits or modifications of the excellencies of his kind.

It is true that varieties of the strongest nature actuate individuals even of the same nation, and under like predicament of spot; acuteness directs application; imagination affords matter for the deeper speculatist; the politician reins the impetuosity of the valiant; and every different force and temper of mind insufficient in itself, seems to strike fire by collision with the proper substance: thus arts flourish; thus science civilises; and thus, men from a very discord of character form the harmony of the social system.

Society

Society will doubtlesly thus perfect itself in proportion to the diversities of its component parts, which by their various combinations and reciprocities, may enlarge the *materia medica* of human weakness, and serve the wants and luxuries, the hopes and vanities, the curiosity and activity of man; and though an isolated nation may from the resources of various character and force of genius within itself, make much progress, may excell in many arts, and push its enquiries far in knowledge; yet cannot it cope with others of more general commerce, and heterogeneous mixture: let China bear testimony to the position; has that vast but sequestered nation made a progress in humanity proportionate to its duration?—Do not the infant colonies of the west—the very republics of yesterday outstrip her in the great career, and boast of theories and inventions she knows not, or knows but weakly? It is the general commerce and intercourse with each other which hath given the people of Europe this sudden superiority; a variety of national character has forced new combinations on that of individuals; and Italian fancy, French wit, English penetration, and German assiduity, have from diverse and distant habitations met, and

united

united their common labors, and connected and modified their several properties, for the furtherance of every art of utility or entertainment.

Attica in the remoteſt antiquity, boaſted ſimilar advantages; ſcarcely had ſhe learnt the firſt rudiments of art and policy, when various colonies acceded to the country, and holding forth a new horn of plenty, enriched her native ſtores with exotic germes of knowledge and civilization.

The religions and the ſciences from the north and from the ſouth hailed each other in this central ſpot: Orpheus brought in the deities of Thrace; and the Saitæ met him, fraught with all the ſuperſtitions, wiſdom, and policy of old Ægypt: the priſtine inhabitants received this colony as a gift of the gods; cheriſhed it; adopted its cuſtoms; not ſatisfied with affording a merely hoſpitable refuge, tended honor and dominion; and finally ſeated the chieftain of theſe exiles on the countries' throne: the myſteries of religion they incorporated with their own; and their own hereditary manners and diſtinctions they gave up, and anew, claſſed themſelves according to the arrangement of duty and honors they were taught by theſe foreign

reign settlers: as in Ægypt, the nation was now triply divided into the distinct classes of the literary noble, the countryman and the artizan—So sudden was the transition from irregular policy, to a system of good order and good government!

The Carians too (whom Herodotus terms the wisest of men) at length forsook their piracy, and fixed themselves on this coast, long the object of their depredations; they soon reconciled themselves to the previous settlers, and at the port Phaleron, laid the foundation of that naval power, which subsequently raised the Athenians to wealth, to conquest, and to empire!

Nor was it to these exotics only that Attica paid the grateful debt of exact and anxious cultivation; in this age of simplicity the human mind not yet refined into depravity, as it saw virtue, acknowledged and rewarded it: in the progression of rulers, we find a Messenian for an act of bravery, called to the Athenian throne; and with him many wanderers from various parts of Greece came to partake his government, and cede somewhat of their native rustic liberty to a system of general comfort and security.

The petty districts of the Peloponnese had now sometime handled the helm of government,
—but

—but with a rude and unskillful force: constant wars harassed them from without, and perpetual dissention at home; and from imbecillity or disgust many yet forsook their native hearth, and went in search of a habitation more favorable to their fears or to their philosophy; and though in the course of human acquirements, the nurseries of these men were far behind-hand with Attica; yet minds rectified from error, and refined by misfortune, proved no useless lesson or unprofitable connexion: sympathy and similitude of lot soon mutually attached these various exiles; the diversity of origin and habitual sentiment and prejudice thence proceeding, naturally led them to think and discourse on their prior state and reciprocal objections; past error and misery sweetened the intercourse with diffidence and complacency; and as the rougher points and irregularities of two surfaces are employed to smooth and perfect each other, so gradually did this commerce destroy the crudities of each national character, and form one compact body of reasonable men, and polished citizens.

A long continuance of plenty and security is too apt to elate the mind, and carry it beyond the nice boundaries of prudence and contented

virtue:

virtue: when a state is from low degrees become thus full of rich and restive blood, better is it than the humour, expend itself in ebullition, than recoil and ferment within, to the detriment of the internal commonweal, and perhaps to its very dissolution and ruin.

At a time when the habits of converse and thought quickened the passions and apprehension; at a time when the minds of men were growing too active for rest, and too turbulent for controul; when the wife and the valiant anew felt and claimed distinctions over their fellows; when the ambition of some and envy of others was succeeding to the virtuous and peaceable emulation of all; the danger of relapsing into anarchy was imminent and great; but fortunately—the shade of chivalry arose, and beckoning each active genius into her circle, preserved the internal state from that annoyance the wanton spirit of the age might seem to portend. Damsels ravished, and damsels rescued, make up the history of this period; not even in the feudal lower age, was enterprize more the delight or admiration of all: the wreath of honor was then first snatched, and separately and distinctly worn from the crown of virtue; whilst the dangers and not motives of the achievement

were

were confidered:——Throughout all Greece, fays Thucydides, arms were in every hand, 'till Athens renewed the example of civilization, and her citizens firſt laid aſide the ſword: ſo many wanderers then poured into Attica, as the only and peculiar feat of permanent and happy councils (continues the fame author) that ſhe too in her turn was forced to colonize, and fend forth her ſupernumeraries to till the fields of Ionia.

Mark the progreſs—Common fecurity was the firſt band of union; indigence inſtructed, intereſt cemented, and foreign population enriched and enlarged the fociety: from long peace and fecurity fprang new diſtinctions among men; influence in private life extended to aſcendancy in the ſtate; individuals grew impatient of reſt and of equality, and ambition like a famiſhed tiger, was recurring to its own litter for fuſtenance and prey, when a providential caſualty directed its activity to external objects; and in the mean time the commonwealth had peace and leiſure, to find theories to its practice, and draw practice from theory—to widen the foundation of the ſtate ſyſtem, and cement it ſo as to withſtand whatever ſhock, till time and progreſſive reaſon ſhould finiſh the building —the glory and bulwark of Greece!

CHAP.

CHAP. IV.

THE natural rights and liberties of mankind were soon felt though late understood; and when, in this state composed of diverse nations and people, the varieties of each had opened the minds of all; when reason and passion had shown a disposition to make stronger and earlier shoots in this heterogeneous soil; the love and fear of power were of the same birth.

From the earliest period of monarchy, the people were ever encroaching on its supremacy; and many of their kings raised from a low degree to the throne, thought much too of their own duties, and their people's claims; their own just subserviency to the interests of the multitude whose sovereignty was merely delegated to their care and fidelity.

Whilst other countries boast a long and successive train of heroes, we find in the list of Athenian kings but very few marked in characters of renown: the spirit of the people was ever in vigilant opposition to that of despotism, and splendid ambition found not means of eluding
the

the caution of the public, and wading into the fields of glory through bloodshed and oppression; thus the servants and not masters of the community, their preheminence of character was in general confined to virtues which were the portion of many, and undistinguished,—as each individual star in the galaxy though still making part of its beauty and its lustre. If any one king attained a brighter and more glorious name than the rest, it was from some act of danger to himself or of benefit to the state, and which would equally have ennobled its meanest constituent; but from Theseus to Codrus we find few remarked for any eccentric exploit.

Codrus paid the debt of nature to his country; and under pretence of deference to the memory of their heroic king, the Athenians permitted none thereafter to bear the same title.

Hitherto the *libido regnum* had full sway and authority; no written laws or definite regulations as yet circumscribed the abuse of power; whatever restrictions might curb its excess, were founded on the comparative fears of the monarch, the pretensions of the eminent, and the impetuosity of the multitude: but the time was now come when institution was to correct the

system

syftem of command and fubmiffion, and fketch out the adequate degrees of each.

Some authors have idly claffed the firft Archons with the Athenian kings, obferving that a change took place in little more than the title of the mafter: were this the fact, ftill was the alteration of moment; even in the moft enlightened ages what prefcriptive devotion hath been paid to mere words!—how much honor and authority have attended a title even when ufurped with the worft of crimes or meaneft of frauds! are there none even in this land of freedom, whofe hearts yet acknowledge the hereditary abjection of their forefathers, and would cancel their very bond of independancy to crouch for their all to fome idol-name?

The word King had in Attica, as elfewhere, a traditionary afcendant over many who knew not the purport of the title, or the individual who bore it; with the name much of this blind veneration ceas'd; and refpect, that great barrier to public liberty being broken down, the paths to an independant commonweal were not lefs open than alluring.

In truth the change of title was not the only one that took place on the death of the patriot Codrus: " the Medontidæ (fays Paufanias) re-
" ceived the fovereignty much abridged of its
" former

"former power, and ultimately made accounta-
"ble to the people for a juſt and due exerciſe of
"the truſt repoſed." What theſe reſtrictions were,
we are not told; but they muſt have been manifold and ſtrong, to have rendered the laſt regulation of any effect; for who ſhall dare to meet the lion in his foreſt? Can deſpotiſm be called to account? The hardy challenger, if ſuch is to be found, muſt prepare for death, or the ſtate for a revolution! but perhaps the proofs are more than preſumptive, that on the eſtabliſhment of the Archons, their ſway was confined to much narrower limits than that of their predeceſſors; and that an accuſation was neither uncommon in itſelf, nor dangerous to the appellant. The uſurper Piſiſtratus pleading as a criminal before the court of the Areopagus ſeems to have had retroſpect to ſome ſimilar cuſtom of the Archons, and to ſeek favor from his citizens by this deference to their prior inſtitutions: other facts might be adduced; but I think the future hiſtory of the commonwealth is itſelf ſufficient proof of what is aſſerted:—on the death of Alcmæon did any commotion ſucceed, when the government was made decennial? Did not the citizens fearleſs of any evaſion of this their new determination, confide the limited ſceptre to the ſame family who had borne it in perpetuity?

petuity? or had any one of these Archons the hardiness or authority to extend the duration of their command? Yet I find not that Charop's office differed from that of his brother Alcmæon save in the confined period of poffeffion.

A ten years command still seemed to preclude too many candidates, and to the ambitious competition of the ploutocracy Athens was indebted for a further step into the regions of freedom: The Archonship was made annual, and the power was divided amongst nine, invested with various duties and authority. This oligarchy severally acting with a vague and indefinite jurisprudence, as various as partial in their decrees, soon gave rise to faction, to party and discontent. The commonalty demanded some surety for their persons and property; the nobles wished to strengthen their order by unanimity; and the alien deprecated the partial judgment which unrestricted might echo to the calls of native affections and domestic interests: thus all united to require written and irrefragable rules of jurisdiction: Draco was summoned by the general voice of his countrymen to be their legiflator; and his Thesmoi (though the few remaining, I think, by no means speak him equal to the sublime trust he was honor'd with) for a time gave quiet and harmony to the republic.

CHAP.

CHAP. V.

THE sophist deep in midnight lucubration exults over the solution of his problem, and looks down on the pursuits of others with derision and contempt: Respect indeed seems due to the operations of the intellect, in preference to the more mechanical labors of the body; but if (as we ought to do) we measure the value of every occupation by its comparative usefulness to society; the recluse studies of many will be discovered to be but a more specious way of trifling, and honest industry will bear the palm over such idle speculations however fanciful or penetrating. Mental researches when directed to proper objects, have the justest claim to our veneration; but let us proportion it to the benefits thence accruing to mankind, nor hallow those ingenious extravagancies, our praise of which hath already allured but too many professionaries of science from its just and useful limits, into some wild and unprofitable search

search, after some truth without consequence, or system without foundation.

Of all employments of the mind, surely that is the worthiest, and as it were divine, which seeks to establish order in society; to humanize the great Leviathan; to adapt the various parts of the vast machine, and nicely fit each spring; where it can best act, each wheel where it can best move, to the intent and good purposes of the general combination; to duely weigh and obviate the friction that might impede, or material which might swerve to the detriment of the diverse parts—till the whole proceed in just and invariable concert!

The legislator must be experienced, to know mankind; and wise,---for he is to direct them; he must be virtuous,—for precepts are to be recommended by example; and brave,—for innovation is to be enforced with courage; and after all, says the younger Pliny,—*Neque cuiquam tam clarum statim ingenium est, ut possit emergere, nisi illi materia, occasio, fautor etiam commendatorque contingat*: To few as these great qualities are allotted, to fewer is given the opportunity of exerting them!

It was soon that the regulations of Draco were found inadequate to the great purpose of harmonising the discordant interests of the citizens

tizens of Athens: The rich and the poor still combated with the respective arms of authority and numbers; and those who were in a middle state of competency, disrelished a situation which was to include them in the conquests of either party, the slaves of a despotic faction, or prey of a lawless multitude.

Arts of every kind had made a quick progress; the pyrates from Caria had introduced the knowledge of navigation; and the parentage of its citizens in foreign countries, had given Athens early notions of profiting of a connexion with diverse and distant parts: Trade soon gave birth to inequalities of opulence and power; and now, in this general mart, this seat of rivalship and commerce, the encreasing love and examples of luxury demanded the readiest and quickest road to wealth: Project might enhance on the profits of trade, and a well concerted scheme suddenly place the lowest citizen on a level with the most opulent; thus many of a voluptuous or ambitious turn, strained their every faculty in some novel and visionary pursuit.

The rich favored this destructive spirit of enterprise, by advancing necessaries for these undertakings; the returns of which being found most precarious, the interest for loans was increased, and gradually the most usurious exorbitancy was tolerated, till in fine even a small debt became the ground-work of an insolvency; and under severe laws of credit, as necessary in a commercial commonwealth, very many were at the mercy of their fellow citizens: it was a law, that the debtor whose pecuniary means were insufficient, was to repay the loan by corporal service; but as the interest of the debt was out of all proportion to the principal, well were it if a discharge of that, and by the severest servitude could appease the taskmaster, and prevent other wanton, and yet legal exercise of his resentment. Under such circumstances some even of the most wealthy, but who had avoided all usurious practices, dreaded the croud of instruments to tyranny, which others of their order kept in unremitting confinement, and which by peculiar favor or kind treatment, might be conciliated to any treachery or usurpation of their ambitious masters: joining with those of the middle state, they sought to anticipate the danger by a new modulation of the commonwealth; they united their efforts to influence the body of the people; the wisdom and virtues of Solon had rendered him eminently conspicuous;

ous; and not (as ufual) by ballot, but by general fuffrage, he was declared Archon and lawgiver.

Solon being afked—" how injury, or injuftice, " might be forbad a place in human fociety ?"—Anfwered—by teaching all to feel the injuries done to each:—to fix fuch focial intereft, fuch reciprocal philanthropy on inftitution;—to direct equally the hopes and fears, equally the reafon and paffions of *all*—to the fame object, to the fecurity of *all*—in a word, wifely to profit of the connexion of felf-love and focial, and by making each man a citizen, to make each citizen a patriot, feems to have been the great object in view throughout the legiflation of Solon.

In the body of the whole people he placed the ultimate authority of debate, for the interefts of the whole were concerned in the decifion: in the order of patricians he centered the executive power, for a liberal education and independance he deemed requifite to office, and their diftinction might give authority to the difcharge of it.

To the nobles he confined the court called Areopagus, and beftowed on it every honor and dignity: to equiponderate the balance, he

on

on the other side constituted a senate annually to be chosen from the several tribes; and in this, were resident the greater power and authority: All matters previous to a reference to the people were herein proposed, argued, and explained; and rejected or dreſt out for public debate, as should seem most fitting and salutary.

As the Areopagus was composed only of the most eminent of the nobles,—of such as had gone the Archonship with credit and applause; so the senate was to be a compound of the best men of the whole community; the candidates lives were strictly examined into by the guardians of their respective tribes, and then again previous to the ballot they were to be approved of by the Archons: under such precautions the reader will observe that the ballot, far from being a ridiculous mode of forming the magistrature, preserved impartiality in the state, gave discontent the colour of irreligion, and to every virtuous and sensible citizen, and to only such, opened a claim to office, and a probability of success.

It was the prætorship and other powers which in after-times were given by suffrage, and not those drawn by lot, which proved ruinous to the republic.

As

As the voice of the senate might be supposed for the most part to have sufficient weight with the people to influence their resolutions, each meaner denizon might seem too little inteterested in, and as it were, estranged from the commonwealth; in order there into give him a self-consequence by public occupation, a judicial capacity was assigned to all whose irreproachable morals and conduct permitted the claim; and their names were drawn by lots for the several juries in the different courts of judicature.

It was ever inculcated that office was not to be courted as giving power and ascendency;—its powers originated in and belonged only to the constitution, and its duties, and duties only, were considered as properly belonging to the magistrate or minister confided in: the more strongly to instill this idea, and to wipe the blot of injustice too from this distinction, each man in office from the Archon to the juryman, received a daily pay for his services and attendance; and thus too the poorer but good citizen, saw not his family distressed from the sacrifice of his private vocation to public duties.

Various were the laws framed more particularly to inculcate, that the state belonged to every man, and every man to the state: the debtor's

effects

effects might be seized, but his person was sacred; for his goods and chattels were private property, but himself belonged to the republic: exception was made in the distrain to implements of husbandry and art; for idleness was at Athens a crime, and to admit crimes of necessity were to foster the most absurd paradox: in all civil and other cases, the parties concerned might chuse their respective advocates; but the advocate was to receive no emolument from his client,---every citizen was his brother, and he was to attend thanks, from their general parent, the commonwealth.

The happiness of all was the object of Solon, and having provided for it by a wise and impartial legislation, he adopted other regulations necessary to the giving vigour and perpetuity to his system.

It has been observed, that he restricted the higher offices of trust to the patrician;—to fix the state on the self-consequence therein of each individual, he made the executive part in all cases responsible to the whole body of the people, for a due exercise of the trust reposed: nay, the very mover of a resolution in the assembly, was liable to be subsequently called to account for his mere proposition; and thence the artful and

interested

interefted man feared to prevail himfelf of an unguarded moment of paffion or prejudice, to influence the populace to decrees of partial tendency, or inconducive to the common welfare: an entrance into the higher order too, was by no means precluded to thofe of the lower clafs, for the qualification was a particular and fixed revenue; and herein hope (ever of more active influence than poffeffion) found new caufe of attachment to the republic, and commerce rejoiced in new incentives to induftry.

To prevent confpiracies of the difcontented or factious, the numbers of guefts at feafts and entertainments were limited; and every where there was free accefs to the public cenfors: if any commotion occurred, neutrality was fubject to fuch fevere and heavy penalties, that action feemed eligible even to the timid, and thus all being concerned, any particular combination might the more readily be crufhed, and the ftate recoil into its priftine conftitution.

It belongs not to this comment to particularize his private laws;—how much they were venerated by antiquity fcarcely an author of note but bears witnefs to! Cicero is a very enthufiaft when he fpeaks of this great legiflator: Livy tells us, that when Pofthumius and others

were

were sent into Greece by the decemvirs, they were ordered—" *inclytas leges Solonis* describere, *aliarum Græciæ civitatum instituta, mores, jataque* noscere:" And Tacitus having enumerated other great lawgivers, proceeds in climax to—Quæsitiores *leges Solonis*.

Scarcely had the system of Solon taken place when the usurpation of Pisistratus frustrated his views by a new establishing the kingly government.

How blind is man! how dark seem the paths through which a beneficent providence often conducts him to success! whilst we peruse the innumerable examples upon record, of slight misfortune conducing to much prosperity;—of the miseries which in the lives of many have unforeseenly proved agents to their superior happiness;—of states elevated to grandeur thro' the improbable means of depression:—we ought not in the apparently evil situation of ourselves or country, to cherish our despondency by specious calculation and presumptuous foresight, but rather look up to the divine will in thankfulness—*Quòd liceat sperare, timenti!*

It was scarcely possible that the habitudes of servitude and command should suddenly be eradicated; and private discontent was more likely

to

to find freſh plea for faction, than to be quieted by new arrangements: injuries take deeper root than benefits; the few were likely to remember the loſs, and the number to be careleſs of the gift: in fine, it was not probable that order ſhould ſo quickly be eſtabliſhed amongſt a people corrupt and at variance; the more perfect the ſyſtem, the leſs conſtant adherence thereto was to be expected from the anarchy of indolence, avarice, ſervility and ambition.

It was the uſurpation of Piſiſtratus that prepared a ſtrong and adequate foundation for the commonwealth of Solon.

Piſiſtratus was the beſt of kings, and by his authority enforcing due obſervance of the private and ſome other inſtitutions of Solon, he taught the great lawgiver's name gradually to be revered; till arrived at a proper maturity, the ſtate profited of an opportunity of innovation, to firmly eſtabliſh the whole body of laws, and the conſtitution ſo wiſely calculated to render them an happy and free people

CHAP

CHAP. VI.

THE ready acquiescence of the ploutocracy in the legislation of Solon, could not proceed but from the impossibility of immediate resistance to a measure they did not expect, and therefore were not provided to oppose.

The remission of debts; the diminution of their power; their previous life of cruelty and injustice, which no act of amnesty could cancel in the book of conscience, however it might preclude public punishment or private insult;—all these, and many other circumstances gave birth to conflicting passions of various bent and force, but all pushing to the subversion of a government, so obnoxious to the prior habits of vice and tyranny.

The manifold dissentients of necessity formed a coalition, and had it not been for the more soaring ambition of some of the party, again had the state recoiled into all the evils of its tyrannous

nous ariftocracy: Lycurgus and Megacles, two of the moft powerful and opulent of the rank of nobles, headed each their refpective parties in contention for the fupreme power; when Pififtratus artfully feized the regal prize from between the unwary competitors.

Of all the paths to ufurpation the moft ready is through the favor of the poorer clafs; their numbers are at once greater, and no individual intereft therein is of fufficient moment to break the combination: their intellect being confined to narrower limits, its feat and bent is the more eafily difcovered by the artful orator; and of nearly equal force and tenor throughout the lift of individuals, he is not at the pains of fearching for and joining the varieties of reafoning fuited to different tempers and minds; and thus is his tafk lefs difficult; and as his art is lefs neceffary, his fallacy is lefs obvious: The paffions too of the multitude are eafily awakened, and undirected by penetration to diftant objects are contented to fympathize with thofe before them, and thus readily are they worked upon by the well-acted part of the defigning demagogue.

Quintilian feems defirous in his delineation of a perfect orator, of entering into competition
with

with the wifeman of the ftoics, by crouding into the catalogue of accomplifhments every virtue and every talent: perhaps Pififtratus approximated the exalted character nearer than any of antiquity; Cicero calls him the Prince of Grecian eloquence, and prefers his powers of fpeaking to thofe of Solon; his wifdom was efteemed fuch, that his name was added to the lift of fages of Greece; Gellius tells us he was the firft that inftituted a public library; and when we remember the liberal arts, let us remember, it was perhaps to the erudition and care of Pififtratus that we owe the prefent exiftence of the Iliad: as a man and as a citizen we have the great law-giver's own affent to his poffeffing the virtues of either in fo eminent a degree, as to leave no room for cenfure except of his ambition to be fupreme; and when vefted with the fupreme power, his conduct was fo moderate, and his regulations fo juft and wife, that each acrimonious reproof of the fame Solon, ftill concludes with the confeffion, that he is yet the beft of kings.

Solon was much indebted to him for every mark of private friendfhip; and his character as a legiflator, owed not lefs to him on the fcore of public honor and veneration; for Pififtratus not only

only adopted and enforced his laws, but recommended them too by the most condescending example, elevating the dignity of the Areopagus by his own public homage and submission to its authority.

Pisistratus was well aprized that habits of power are not readily foregone, and he accordingly banished the chief of the Aristocracy from the city: he well knew that the idle would be meddling and tumultuous, and therefore necessitated every denizon to some trade or occupation; but as he likewise foresaw that commerce was not to be fostered but by a spirit of equality, and national freedom incompatible with his views of government, he directed the attention and industry of his subjects to as yet much neglected agriculture.—Perhaps too he had the penetration to judge the career of the Athenians to have been hitherto, too hasty; and remanded them to their primitive occupation, as not being yet sufficiently mature,—to grace injustice with policy, to adorn corruption with elegance, *and to clothe, as it were, the nakedness of vice.*

Pisistratus underwent many reverses of fortune, but the vicissitudes of his power not being sufficiently particularized by any historian to

give

give—"*the spirit of character or event,*" the stating of the mere outside facts comes not within the purpose of this comment.

Were we acquainted with a minute detail relative to Megacles' connecting himself with his competitor Lycurgus, to expel their common enemy; his recal of that enemy to worst his prior opponent; the second expulsion of Pisistratus to gratify family resentment, and again his resumption of the regal seat,—had we (I say) a just and particular account of each fact and agent of this wondrous little history;—so many passions, so many arts of political intrigue might be found to center in it, that perhaps would it merit not a chapter but a volume!

As much virtue, and as much wisdom have often been employed to effect a purpose in common life, as to manage a ministerial business; and the memoirs of one whose hours are checquered with the functions and difficulties of at once a public and private station, most justly engage the avidity of the reader: how much then would his attention be fixed to the interesting lesson of a whole commonweal, repeatedly wavering to domestic incidents, and public and private interests reciprocally influencing, and depending on, the one the other!

CHAP.

CHAP. VII.

SO firmly had Pififtratus eftablifhed the kingly power, that on his deceafe, without commotion it peaceably defcended to his children; and happily for Athens they were not lefs heirs to their father's virtues and wifdom, than to his throne.

Whatever might be the participation in government bequeath'd to the other brothers, ftill fuperiority of merit as well as the rights of elderhood, placed the chief authority in Hipparchus; who having under fuch a preceptor as Pififtratus imbib'd an early tafte for the polite arts, purfued them through every branch of the mechanic to the more liberal, and to the moft exalted: he planted and waled in the Acàdemia for the ufe and difquifitions of the philofopher: he enlarged and emended the compilation of Homer's rhapfodies undertaken by his father; and to awaken new emulation among the Mufes, his patronage was held forth to every fervant of Parnaffus;—

and Simonides and Anacreon were his friends: the city was a great part rebuilt and every where adorned under his infpection; and as the progrefs of art difplayed itfelf in the beauteous appearance of Athens, fo equally did fcience fhow its influence in the polifhed demeanor of the Athenians.

An eccentric genius hath contended that a delicate and highly finifhed civilization is equally deftructive to the virtues, and to the happinefs of mankind; and that a life of inftinct were preferable to the fomuch-boafted acquifitions of fociety: without entering into the trite arguments relative to a ftate of nature, let me obferve, that improveability being one diftinguifhing quality of man, it not only indicates that this fanciful fyftem of ignorance is to the laft degree paradoxical, but implies too, the intention of the creating and fuperintending being, to fix the happinefs of man in the activity of his faculties; and furely it is in polifhed fociety, that the exercife of them may be pufhed to the greateft extent and variety, and be attended with the leaft danger and inconvenience: The polite world in the courfe of its refinements hath adopted a certain though indefinable code for familiar conduct, which without faying how far thou mayft go,

tells

tells thee when thou art to go no further; and thus without taking vivacity from difcourfe, or argument from debate, conciliates the intetcourfe of man with man by a reciprocal and prefcriptive condefcenfion; and to the modern cynic let me remark, that from deficiency of fuch rules deducted from polifhed humanity, many centuries even of our own æra have been blackened with fuch extravagancies of vice and cruelty, as thofe of a more liberal age would fhudder at the mere recital of.

Can we fuppofe, when from the catalogue of emperors and kings, fo many are to be felected who began their reign with juftice, and clos'd it in tyranny.—Can we fuppofe, that for years they artfully concealed their depravity, and from the firft internally acknowledged the immoral tendencies which covered their future days with fhame and ruin?—Rather am I inclined to believe, that the plenitude of power hath been the firft caufe of corruption,—that the moft virtuous of defpots have at fome finifter hour unwarily learn'd to admit adulation, thence to deduct arrogance, and thence, (whilft they no longer duly poized the fcale of relative duties and merits) unfeelingly to regard the wrongs or miferies of thofe imploring their juftice or beneficence.

Hip-

Hipparchus was of the number whose virtues ceded to the baneful influence of unbounded power; from a vain attempt to corrupt the morals of Harmodius, he directed his attack to the chastity of the young man's sister; the youth inflamed with rage at the repeated insult, told his story, and declared his desires of vengeance to his preceptor Aristogeiton; Aristogeiton sympathized in his pupil's just resentments, and with ardor joined in a conspiracy to assassinate Hipparchus.

We are informed that Hipparchus three days previous to his death, saw a vision which foretold him the consequences of his injustice: is it to be wondered at, that remorse found a spectre for a tyrant;—or that an evil conscience should start at a shadow, and lend its fears the spirit of prophecy!—*verane hæc affirmare non ausim, interest tamen exempli ut vera videantur!*

Harmodius fell an immediate victim to his revenge; Aristogeiton was seized and reserved for the sentence of Hippias, brother and successor to the deceased king: to every question, even when on the rack, he answered with the most determined fortitude; and being asked by the incensed monarch the names of his accomplices in the conspiracy, he directed his revenge to the most faithful adherents of the tyrant, and by firmly

and

and invariably recording his dearest inmates in the accusation, blackened every future hour with horror and suspicion.

The connexion of Aristogeiton and Harmodius, of the old man and the young, or (as the Greeks termed them) of the lover and the beloved, is so well known, and yet has been so often and so much misconstrued, that a short digression on the subject may not be improper to this essay. That such connexions were universally in practice we have the authority of all antiquity to prove: in many the most virtuous states, and particularly in Sparta, it was infamous for a youth not to be the object of affection to some one of maturer age; and yet Ælian tells us that—*" if such intercourse were polluted with ought of criminality, exile and even death were the penalties of the offence:* but had we not this and many other authorities for the purity of these attachments;—were we not told of the chaste predilection of Socrates for Alcibiades, and of many other great men for some young pupil or follower—can we suppose (and some have supposed) that these friendships were still sullied with immorality;—and that mere custom in a word could universally give the most horrid and
dis-

disguftful vice a preference over the deareft and moft neceffary inftinct of nature?

I am perfuaded that the prohibition of the ufe of boys to flaves, merely alluded to the particular but pure amity above defcribed, and was founded on the too great advantages enfuing fuch correfpondence—advantages of inftruction and liberal document, which the young domeftic could imbibe, but to the prejudice of that humility fo neceffary to fervitude, in a ftate wherein the flaves fo much out-number'd the citizens.

—To them and their advancement what a happy futurity was in view, whilft each younger denizon was inftructed by the conduct and counfels of fome adopted father, who was to inftil into him the love of virtue and of his country, and then blefs his work, and exultingly live over again in the public and moral merits of his pupil!

Nothing more conduces to vice than the too general commerce of the young with the young: reafon in fuch fociety is deafened by clamour, loft in impetuofity, or fubdued by paffion; nor doth it refift the ufurpation whilft in example it finds a ready palliative to the fufferance: but the intercourfe of thofe of different times of life
me:

meliorates the characters of either, tempering the morofenefs of age and the petulance of youth.

That thefe very intimate connexions were fometimes of vicious tendency, may be allowed; but the contamination fhould be confidered in the light of exception, and not of general and approved practice.

CHAP.

CHAP. VIII.

AS the conduct of the two former kings had served to promote a love of order and a habit of polished demeanor, calculated to obviate all danger of licentiousness or anarchy should a state of liberty ensue; so did the odious tyranny of their successor make that liberty the darling wish of every Athenian.

Incensed at the death of his brother, and alarmed at the informations of Aristogeiton, Hippias showed vengeance the bloodiest paths of cruelty, and as suspicion found him objects, remorse envenom'd, and practice hardened his mind to a familiarity with the horridest scenes of massacre and oppression.

His subjects were vexed with new and accumulating imposts, and every man's mereft competency was drained, and his necessities postponed, to the luxuries and excess of a vicious court; whilst each noble, eminent for wealth or merit, hourly was in danger of falling a victim to the fears of the despot, or to the avarice of his adherents;

herents: many under such circumstances voluntarily left their native country, and many were driven into banishment to pamper the creatures of the palace with confiscations.

Every passion united to urge these exiles to a recovery of their lost fortunes and country; and a connexion of one of the proscribed families with the Pythian priestess happily suggested the means of success: this minister of the oracle at their instigation interested the Lacedæmonians in the enfranchisement of their city; constantly replying to their every demand with the previous injunction to deliver Athens from the tyranny. Whether from the ambitious desire of some pretence to get footing on the other side the isthmus, or other political, or perhaps really religious, motive, the Spartans readily promised the assistance required, and sent an armament (but of small force) which was worsted by Hippias and his auxiliaries.

No longer was the contention directed by the meek efforts of generous Piety;—national pride was concerned;—the Spartans felt the indignity of the repulse, and to efface all memory of the defeat, repeated the attack with redoubled force, and sent their king Cleomenes to head, and en-

sure

sure success to the expedition. Fortunately they intercepted the children and family of Hippias attempting to evade the dangers of the siege, nor would they deliver up these precious hostages to the king, but on the condition of his immediately giving up the citadel and abdicating the sovereignty. Thus was Athens freed from the usurping family of Pisistratus.

Clisthenes, who was a chief agent in the revolution, gained great credit thereby with his countrymen; and on his return rivetting the affections of his fellow-citizens by a specious display of moderation and ability, his influence over the people became so great, that his virtue was dazzled with the glaring and open prospect of power; and he no longer saw, that not to abuse a merited ascendency in a free state, was the noblest fame; and the most glorious object of ambition, to unite the command of one's-self, with that over others: on stretching his hand out to the sceptre, it however met a competitor for the grasp: Isagoras revived the opposition to the family of Megacles, of whom Clisthenes was a lineal descendant; and on the faith of foreign assistance he too put in a claim to the throne: during the prior expedition, the Spartan leader had been his guest, and in ancient times such hospitality was

ever

ever after, a plea for favor or afliftance, as ftrong as the feelings of a long and approved amity. Cleomenes gave a ready ear to the entreaties of his hoft, and immediately turning his arms towards Athens, expelled Clifthenes and his party; and having purfued them beyond the boundaries of the country, returned to mafter the city, and model its conftitution and ftate to the will and pleafure of Ifagoras; but the Athenians had favoured the momentary tafte of liberty, and were already become too high-minded to tamely yield their necks to the yoke, they had fo lately fhaken off; indignant at the attempt, they generally accorded to reprefs the Spartan, and punifh the few unworthy citizens who had joined thefe foreigners, and who abetting the invafion of their newly recovered liberties, vilely had prefer'd the name of Partizan, to that of Patriot.

Cleomenes and his forces quickly gave way to the impetuous fpirit of newly acquired freedom; forced into the citadel, they for a while relied on the ftrength of the place, but at length the determinate valour and affiduity of the befeigers enforced a capitulation: the Lacedæmonians were difmiffed in fafety; but the Athenian delinquents were to a man put to death,—a pro-

pitious

pitious sacrifice to the ascendant day-star of liberty!——the example was efficacious:—— Clisthenes returning from his second exile, coincided with the spirit of his fellow citizens; and with emulative ardour abetted the establishment of the commonwealth of Solon.

Pore over each system from the Stagyrites, to the politician's letter of the day, still of every form of government you will observe the democratic to have met with the most universal censure; but perhaps it may be found, that this disapprobation, general as it is, proceeds less from the faults of such republican constitution than other latent cause imperceptibly influencing its opponents.

The aristocratic part of society seems to be the body of men of superior or cultivated intellect, and the argument falling of course to their disquisition, the commonalty of mankind are not likely to be treated with a consideration divested of partiality or prejudice;——" the *first* builds on a conscious superiority over the multitude; and the *second* takes experience of its insufficiency and incertitude as an equally sound corner stone for a stable and firm superstructure:" Who (says one of these monarchs of an easy chair)—" who ought to govern, if not the

" chosen

"chosen few whose rank and opulence have af-
"forded the means of education, whose powers
"of intelligence have been brought forth, and
"whose capacity unerring in self-conduct, seems
"so fitted to regulate that of others?—Shall
"we indiscriminately trust our fortunes to the
"indigent, our honors to the mean, or our
"private happiness, and the public weal to
"an ignorant multitude, whose ears lead but to
"their passions, affording a ready road to the
"rhetorical agent of domestic treasons or of
"foreign interests?"——Soft, Soft, my good
Sir—you have built truly your fairy-castle, and
would now brutify each inhabitant of the domain
with all the whimsical severity of a magician in
a Romance! the intellects of mankind originally
are of much nearer equality, than you are willing to suppose;—the diversities, whence you
are about to deduce the argument of this specious declamation, proceed from the casualties
around you;—to suddenly form a democratic
body of the heterogeneous mass you have in
view, were absurd indeed; but the absurdity is
the creature of your own brain: when you
again examine the merits of this form of government, candidly reject such misleading pre-
mises;

mifes; confider a democracy when well regulated on its beft principles, and well eftablifhed on the happieft practice;——with equality of power, as far as policy *fhould* concede, fuppofe equality of intellect as far as nature *will* admit, unaffifted by other afcititious advantages than fuch as are open to he whole people; every argument refpecting their infufficiency will in fuch cafe fall to the ground, for thefe advantages are not lefs great than general:—may not a conftant attention to public affairs form the minds of many, as of one, to a verfatility and penetration fitted for all the variety and difficultiesof bufinefs?——Without being ftatefmen, may not very many learn well to judge of ftatefmen?—— And this is all that is neceffary, for merit will have the means of forcing itfelf into office, through public notice and efteem; and on fuch ought its fole claim to reft.

But you talk of the fubferviency of a popular audience to every fallacy of an artful orator!— and do you really then think that a multitude dailily accuftomed to all the artifice and force of harangue, is to be claffed with a modern croud, opening wide their eyes, and mouths too, to the declaimer, as if ignorant with which fenfe to receive the novel tafte of eloquence?—

Pericles

Pericles truly pleads to the paſſions!—aye—to thoſe of fame and public ſpirit:—Demoſthenes pleads to the paſſions!—he lived in the decline of the republic, yet con over his Olynthiacs or Philippics, and tell me if he hath attempted to rouſe ought other emotion than of virtue and patriotiſm!——theſe in a learned and free ſtate (and a free ſtate will be a learned one) are the only paſſions at all times open to the orator; and touching theſe he had more nearly recalled the commonwealth to its firſt energy and principles, than could have done any merely ſyſtematic debater.

Thrives not ſtate opulence on commerce? Public conſequence and dignity on domeſtic union?—And that union on a ſociality of ſelf-intereſt?—and boaſts not a free republic a ſuperiority in theſe reſpects over any other whatever?

A warm advocate for the liberties of mankind,—(liberties, which political inſtitution ought ſurely to medicate with the tendereſt hand, nor wantonly corrode or amputate) I may perhaps appear bold in aſſerting that a democracy in the *high perfection of its eſtabliſhment*, is the ſtate the beſt calculated for general happineſs, and that the true and good objection to it, proceeds

not

not from the vices of such constitution, but from the unavoidable brevity of its career.

The primary authority is resident in the many; but of force the executive power must be delegated to the few: the *first* is in the hands of the people, whose will being once determined and promulgated, necessity from day to day more rarely calls for their interposition; the *second* entrusted to their agents, requires unremitted exertion; as the one power becomes dormant, the latter encreases in vigilance; till at length the importance of the state yields to the consequence of private men, and the servant of the public directs the legislation he should obey, whilst the individual reaping influence from the magistracy, reciprocally communicates that ascendancy to his office: thus gradually the constitutional balance is lost, and the commonwealth, whatever of its laws or exterior forms it may for a while retain, hath quickly deviated from the equal and free spirit which characterised the original institution; which at once gave to the state moderation and force, at once ensured to the community peace and virtue at home, and consequence and victory abroad.

Machiavel.

Machiavel obferves in the firft chapter of the third book of his difcourfes, that the moft perfect political arrangement is that which hath fomething in its effence fitted to obviate the diffolution of the ftate, by occafionally recalling it to the firft principles of its inftitution: of this advantage a democracy feems incapable.

When once fuch ftate is affected, the difeafe is not in the head that plans, or heart that wills, or hand that executes;——the whole mafs is generally difordered, nor is there a found part through which the blood may return in a purer ftate to medicate the more corrupted: The peftilence fpreads through the whole body at once, and with that progreffive and fure venom pervades to the very vitals of the conftitution, that to attempt a cure were vain;——to ward off the infection, or to obviate antidotes to the firft poifon of it, may not be fo forlorn a hope. In a monarchy it is from the vitiated morals of its conftituents that government becomes infected: in a democracy the diforder originates in government; for the people muft become idle to become vicious; and muft firft lofe attention to the commonwealth, to have leifure for diffolutenefs and ruin in their private capacities.

Knowing then to what evil, and to what part the preventative should be directed, is there a panacea of sufficient efficacy to ensure success? Surely not!—perhaps the most promising was the species of exile adopted in various republics of yore:——the petalism of Argos and Syracuse, the ostracism of Athens.

What ingratitude to proscribe the virtue that hath long labored for the public weal!---what folly to banish the man whose abilities may be as they have been, the support of the state! what ill-policy, to send to foreign climes at once so useful a friend, and so dangerous an enemy? --Such are the objections which occur on the immediate and first view of the subject, but they must as quickly yield to the stronger reasons in favor of the institution.

It from time to time snatched a dangerous prop from their affairs, and bade the people awaken to their own support and welfare; it made men wary of preheminence, and often taking somewhat from the evergrowing matter of the executive scale, anew balanced the commonwealth.

Public protection implies particular submission, and he who subscribes to fixed ordinances or laws, by seeking security under their shelter,

hath

hath no right to deprecate their penalties or precautions.

No character in a free and equal community can be of sufficient eminence to supersede the interests of the state, without danger that at some sinister period, those interests may be sacrificed to some partial or self-consideration: in as much as the whole outweighs the part, it is proper therefore to have the maxim ever in view,—" that particular should cede to general welfare; and that an individual pays but a just debt to his country, were even life the demand."

But it is not the secession of the old statesman or experienced veteran, fraught with politics and discipline, a loss to his country; and perhaps its enemy?

With respect to the pretended ability and knowledge, the superiority is more dangerous than useful; in a wholesome republic (and we are not now talking of one already corrupted) a sound and plain understanding is the most faithful, and surely an adequate, guide in the straight road of virtuous administration; and whoever talks of the necessarily difficult and crooked paths of government, is to be suspected of meaning treachery on the way, and is to be guarded against, as one desirous of bewildering those he is hired to direct; that his infufficiency may be efs apparent, or treafons more fecure.

That the oftracifm might appear to fome, and might fometimes be an unmerited perfecution;— and that, in the bitternefs of refentment and difguft, an alienation of good-will, might attend a good man on his departure from the commonwealth, was indeed to be apprehended: every circumftance was ftudied therefore to mitigate the evil, property was preferved and remitted during the banifhment, its time was limited, and the very exile was honor.

CHAP.

CHAP. IX.

THE diftinctions or authorities on which man founds his claim to dominion over other creatures were of little moment, had he not the means of enforcing fubjection and obedience: for this power he relies not on the firm texture of bone or of finew; his ftrength depends not on the frame of his body, but on the etherial fpirit which animates it,—on free volition exercifing intellect, and reciprocally intellect tutoring choice, till from the joint activity refult force of thought, ingenuity, forefight, and courage which is no other than felf-confidence deduced from the prior acquifitions.

The more the mind is practifed in this internal or home-education,—— the more varieties are left to its deliberation and to its choice, the more elevated and perfect will it become; and the greater fuperiority will it give over all other animals, whofe faculties being confined to fixed and particular limits, are not able to cope with thofe who indefinitely can encreafe their own,

or

or command extraneous forces to master in contention, or assert in sovereignty

The same circumstances which distinguish man, and make all other creatures abject slaves to his appetite and pleasures, occasion too a difference in the same species; and relatively elevate or abase an individual, and even a whole people in proportion as mental advantages shall have been their respective lot.

In a despotic government, supposing even the administration to be just and wise, still must an inferiority in the point alluded to, be unavoidable; whilst the higher class grow enervate in over-abundance, and the poorer multitude are depressed to a mere communion with the glebe; the minds of this society cannot improve by the wholesome education of general exigency working with general liberty; and long as the success of the number rests on the quality of its constituents, the Tartar will dethrone the Chinese, the savage will conquer the peasant, the freeman the slave.

As the genius and spirit of men become torpid or lost, as it were, under the uncontrolable command of one, it is natural to suppose that an opposite arrangement will be of use to them, and that they will become superior by associating

ing in such a manner, as least to coerce the freedom of will, or hebetate by disuse the powers of mind in each individual; and a republic will most effectually answer this important purpose, the constitution of which favors the equality and independance of each, as far as may be compatible with the safety and union of all; of this let the Athenians be my example: " They, (says Herodotus) when under the
" controul of their kings, were of no account in
" the eye of Greece, but immediately on the
" dissolution of the tyranny, they became great,
" and by far greater, than the people which
" had hitherto held them in so little estima-
" tion."

It may perhaps be observed, that this change looks too sudden to agree with the previous theory;—that the Athenians seem rather inspired than taught;—rather elevated by some instantaneous, than chronical advantage; for they appear to have anticipated all the progressive wisdom of council, on the first emergency; and all the energy of action in their first enterprize: let it be remembered, that this people had been meliorated by vicissitude, and the salutary lesson of transient evil, rather than benumbed by the oppressions of a long tyranny;

that,

that, some were even sufficiently aged to remember the prior times of liberty, and joyfully acknowledge the star which brightened the evening of their day, to have been the same which gave glory to its birth;—many had passed in exile the interval of usurpation; and all had some particle of the spirit of their fore-fathers yet left;—some tale to tell of the miseries of slavery, and of the blessings of freedom;—some hereditary reasoning on private rights and public duties. To this be it added, that the first outset of a republic is ever marked with peculiar force and vigour:—as the limbs newly-unshackled, so the mind liberated from the weight of imperious coercion, springs with fresh elasticity and ardour to every object of activity: the people look up to their new compact; the sentiment precedes the principles of freemen; and they first support, they know not why, what they afterwards find every reason to support: the spark of patriotism first catches, or rather electrically pervades the whole band, nor prematurely fails till progressive virtue and wisdom give it substance to feed on, and extend itself.

The Spartans when they listened to the advice of the oracle and freed Athens from the despotism tifm of the family of Pififtratus, perhaps acted from religion; or perhaps, and more probably were influenced by some political motive: That selfish state (for selfish we shall find it throughout the whole course of Grecian History) was never actuated by principles of philanthropy or satisfied with the sentiment of disinterested protection!

It is to be presumed that some error in policy occasioned their ready compliance with the injunctions of the Pythian priestess; for soon as they saw the tendency of the exploit,—soon as they found that freedom was a gift incompatible with retribution,—that this singular present placed the obliged at a distance from the donor, and admitted not of the vulgar forms of submissive acknowledgment,—They repented them of the hasty interposition, and of having adopted a measure, which, they too late perceived, instead of rendering the Athenian people subordinate, from gratitude to them; or weak, from divisions among themselves;—had raised a spirit of union and self-confidence which portended rivalship of character and dominion: and be it remarked, that when Cleomenes again unsheath'd the sword, no reverence of the will of Heaven withheld his hand from annoying the people he had been ordered to succour and save:--thus quick-

ly

ly at Lacedæmon seems the happy age to have passed over, when (in the words of Livy)—
"*nondum hæc, quæ nunc tenet fecu'um negligentia deûm venerat, nec interpretando sibi quisque jusjurandum et leges aptas faciebat, sed suos potius mores ad ea accomodabat!*"

The Athenians saw and prepared for the impending storm; every where they sought assistance, and even sent to the Persian to proffer their friendship and alliance, and ask an honourable and free support in this their distress: the king questioned with surprise the ministers of this new people, and finally observed that it became them better to talk of homage, than of equal amity, before the Lord of Asia;—that he might be induced to protect them as servants, but could not deign to serve them as allies: the ambassadors unwarily condescended to promise—" earth and water, the " abject acknowledgment required; but on their return to Athens their conduct was censured, and the terms of assistance unanimously rejected.

The Bæotians had now penetrated into Attica on one side; the Chalcidenses were depopulating the coasts; and the Spartan army composed of the chief youth of the state, and inspirited by the presence of their two kings, had pass'd the Isthmus.

mus. The Athenians contemning a merely defensive part, march'd from their city, and prepared to affault the enemy with vigour: the numbers, difcipline, and valour of the Spartans demanded their firft attention, and to them they directed their firft onfet. The Spartans awaited not the attack: their kings Cleomenes and Demaratus differing with refpect to the invafion, or to the conduct of it, the diffenfion fo infected the whole army, that it was not thought expedient in this divided ftate to truft a battle; and they, and their allies precipitately withdrew to their refpective homes; and left the Athenians at liberty to repel the Bæotians and attack Chalcis, both of which expeditions were crowned with fuccefs, and Athens grew up in renown and confequence.

CHAP

CHAP. X.

CIVIL Liberty consists in the secure possession of a particular station and property, not to be affected but by the dissolution of the state which ascertains and ensures them: when a form of government circumscribes the latitude of concession to its subjects of equal rights and participation,—*civil liberty is confined*; when its policy and laws are inadequate to regular administration,—*civil liberty is insecure:* the pretensions of a just and wise legislation are so to modulate its force and its security, and so to provide for general ease and happiness, as to leave as little controul for the free-spirited, and as little licentiousness for the man of a quiet and homely turn, to make the subject of anxiety,—as are compatible with each other, and as absolute necessity requires.

Men of an improved genius and capacity will yet sometimes push their idea of polity to a refinement, calculated to disgust them with any institution they may be born subject to; and men too in the extremities of an hot and active, or of a peaceable and domestic spirit, will find wherewithal to colour their situation with discontent, and deprecate the controul of government or licentiousness of the people, respectively as they are fitted for enterprize or quiet,—for the forum of Rome, or farm at Tibur.

It is certain that no dissatisfaction with the constitution of his country, can authorise an individual to plot an innovation, ever pregnant with danger to the whole community; and that the necessity must be very obvious and pressing,—and the authority of very many must assent, to make any plea for commotion good and adequate.

But happiness, it will be said, is the great end of all political ordonnance or arrangement;— that states may not be of the best institution, that even those of the best may have deviated from their first principle; and surely it is equally hard for a polished and wise man to be aggrieved by the errors of a savage ancestor; or to stand with his head under a ruin, because in a better state it had been a comfortable habitation to his forefathers. This reasoning will have weight in every country which permits not a free egress from its dominion; where such migration is restricted, the canon is unjust, and agrees not with the

great

great axiom—"*Lex est summa ratio*"—for reason favors the contentment and good of *each*, when it interferes not with that of *any*.

That a body of men may leave their native country, and that so doing they withdraw themselves from the parent state, its protection and its powers, I think questions so inseparable, that had not a contrary mode of reasoning been of late much and often enforced,—I should suppose the argument too obvious to necessitate the detail: assuredly those who depart on a conditional expedition, as they are benefited, so are they obligated by the conditions thereof; but the voluntary exile who seeks refuge in the storms of the ocean, and trusts his body to foreign climates and exotic diet; who forgoes the delights of habit, and sweets of long connexion, who flies from so many attachments to so much danger,— flies not from dislike to his paternal glebe or private sociality,—it is from supposed or real grievance of subjection that he escapes, and if the imperious rule is to pursue him to his retreat, the permission to quit the shore is at best trivial and insulting.

The Colony embarking for a region of fixed and regulated society, of course must acquiesce in the previous compact; but landing on a yet unapappropriated spot, have surely as just a right to adopt the system of association, their prejudices or wisdom may suggest.

This was the reasoning of old, and was supported by the demeanor of the ancient repuplics towards the various settlements formed in distant parts by their distgusted or necessitous citizens; for necessity, or from over-population or from other casualties incident to society, might often and perhaps most frequently occasion many to seek other fortunes and another country. On the motives of quitting the original people, depended their successive favor and partial protection (for that partiality may actuate and attach very large and removed societies, this, and in confutation of Dr. Price every history will evince) —and the Colony had a conditionally respected plea for the tender and gratuitous interference of the mother-country, in all cases of exigency and danger.

The cities of Ionia had been conquered and annexed by Cræsus to the kingdom of Lydia, and with Lydia fell into the hands of the Persian: still however they remembered them of their origin, and the commonwealths of their parent Greece newly liberated from their several dynasties, instilled a sentiment of emulation and

in-

indignant shame, which at a favourable crisis might have given birth to a revolution. Miltiades of Athens who had newly thence led a Colony to the Cherfonese, judged that crisis to be arrived:—Darius with all the chiefs and best youth of Asia were employed in the conquest of Scythia; to facilitate the expedition, with great labor and art a bridge had been effected over the Danube, and thither the army was now directing its retreat from the snows and famine of the North: the pass was guarded but by a small detachment, and Miltiades proposed to the chiefs of the Greek settlements, to master the guard, and then breaking down the bridge, to leave Darius and his troops to perish in the colds and dearth of Scythia; and thus destroying at once the tyrant and the instruments of his tyranny, at leisure to form such establishments as were consonant to their ideas of justice, or claims to liberty.

The aristocracies and petty tyrants of this district felt their private interests clash with this hardy proposal; and Histiæus of Miletus particularly remarking to his fellow-despots—" that his and their authority existed but in subordination to the Persian, and that nullifying the lieutenancy of his power, they gave up their own;

—the

—the scheme of Miltiades met with general disapprobation, and perceiving himself to be no longer of service to his own, or any other Colony, he returned to a private situation in his native Athens.

He had however awaken'd the spirit of the Asiatic Greeks, and left them prone to revolt, whenever the opinion of their leaders should cede to the measure; and soon they did cede from factious and selfish passions, what they had denied to more generous and public views, and when the happy opportunity was past, engaged in a contest as dishonorable from motive as ruinous in consequence.

Aristagoras, who moved by private interests and disaffection had been the chief instigator of the rebellion, recurred to Sparta for assistance; but his declamation was ill-suited to the iron assembly of Lacedæmon; an appeal to philanthropy and the sentimental claims of a distant affinity, a tale of distress, and the conscience of a noble kindness, and disinterested protection, were topics better fitted for an audience that respected the softer passions of humanity: to Athens he next applied, and there was received with all honor, and hospitality; succour was unanimously voted, and quickly an armament of

G   twenty

twenty sail was made ready to join the confederate forces: this exertion was the more glorious for Athens, as she was at that very period in expectation of a powerful attack on her own people and country. Cleomenes nurtur'd a rooted enmity, nor yet forewent the idea of ruining the republic that had so often worsted and disgraced him: in hopes that some partizans of Hippias might yet be found in Attica to give a treacherous welcome to his invasion, he purposed making that tyrant the instrument of his vengeance; and inviting him to the Peloponnese, promised to reinstate him in the power he had been the means of depriving him of: the Achæans and other allies of Sparta were however previously to be consulted; a congress was called, and the result of the debate unexpectedly proving inimical to their designs, o'erwhelmed the king and his protected fugitive with confusion and disappointment. Sosicles of Corinth particularly inveighed against the horrors and injustice of tyranny; reproved the rancour of Cleomenes, and chid the Lacedæmonians for favouring a system of oppression in other countries, the establishment of which, they so well knew the evils of, and so well guarded against at home; and in fine peremptorily told them, they were not to expect, that Corinth (whose delegate he was) would further

ther abett a scheme of despotism which (in their own state) too fatal experience had fully evinced was replete with danger and iniquity.

The other ministers coincided with the opinion of Sosicles, and deaf to all menace or intercession, returned peaceably to their respective countries.

Hippias frustrated of his views of succour from the Peloponnese, withdrew to Asia, and profiting of the resentment borne to the Athenians from the support given to the rebellious provinces, persuaded the king to countenance his pretensions to the goverment of Attica: it was at this time that the armament of the colonies attacked and burnt the city of Sardis, and Darius exasperated by the success, vow'd vengeance to the hardy interposition of the Athenians, and gave readier ear to the proffers and entreaties of Hippias.

CHAP.

CHAP. VIII.

MAN *is but what he knows*—says my Lord Verulam; the extent then of his knowledge is that of his excellence, to the attainment of which opportunities of acquisition must coincide with the capacity thereof, and it is not alone the primary circumstances of birth the peculiar rareness of the spirits or quality of their channels, or what else to be acted on by climate or other natural casualty, that can singly elevate the human character, but a further and more refined combination of influences is requisite;—of influences originating not from the material but mental world, not from the temperature of soil or air, or even temperament of parents;—but from the pre-established order of society,—the prescriptive objects of its ingenuity, study, emulation, or esteem. The advantages of *country* in a physical sense, it will readily be granted are not alone equivalent to those of *country* under the political purport of the word; it yet rests

for

for confideration,—how far thefe may agree?—Whether the vertical funs which (according to many ancient and modern fophifts) are fo favorable to a finer texture of the brain, are not oppreffive to its further ftrength and energy?—Whether quicknefs is not incompatible with ftability?—And as man is not fo much excellent from the gift of poffeffing as from the faculty of acquiring, whether the retentive and progreffive powers incident to thofe born under lefs brilliant fkies, give not in the courfe of time and things, a national fuperiority made and ftrengthened by gradual and improved accumulation, which the more vivacious children of the fun muft ever look up to in defpair?—the moft etherial genius born to the community finding no previous common ftock whence to draw inftruction,—no previous bafis whereon to build or improve fyftems for the ufe of, and to further again the progrefs of, pofterity? Avoiding a too long and digreffive train of reafoning, I leave it to the reader's ingenuity to feek, and fupply thefe queries with, a ready affirmative;—to deduct levity from fancy, and ignorance from inaction,—to mark the paffions born of indolence ftifling reafon in its birth; and then to acconnt,—why eaftern genius hath gleam'd in metaphor, and not fhone in poem;

em;—why fancied, and not thought in science;—grafting the firſt ſhoots of knowledge, why left it to others to mature the fruit;——and (touching home to the ſubject) to develope why the people of Aſia dreading the recondite theories and active practice of republicaniſm, have ever ſought, and do ſtill ſeek ſhelter from the diſtreſs of employ and pain of thought, under torpid ſubmiſſion to a deſpot.

Throughout the annals of mankind, I know not a period more fully demonſtrative of the influence of government on men, and of clime on both, than the times of conteſt between Greece and Perſia!

If hiſtory is philoſophy teaching by example,—never did ſhe teach in a more nervous ſtrain, a leſſon of contempt for tyranny, and of love and admiration of a ſtate of freedom!

Darius needed not the ſlave's admonition who was ordered every morning and evening to remember him of Athens; Hippias was a too vigilant incendiary to omit any occaſion of making the king's reſentment ſubſervient to his own intereſts and deſigns.

As ſoon as the rebellion in Ionia was quelled, and the Perſian freed from inteſtine commotion could ſafely lead his forces abroad, the aſſiduity

ity of Hippias prevailed, and Darius sent his ministers to demand homage of the diverse states of Greece, and particularly to deliver his mandate to Athens, to submit at discretion to his power, and to receive Hippias as his delegate: the Athenians not satisfied with treating this embassy with contempt, strove in other parts too to procure it a similar reception; and if any city yielded tokens of submission from motives of lucre or fear, they plainly declared that neutrality was not admissible, and that all who entered not into the common cause with the ardour of friends, were to be regarded as enemies.

The Æginetans were among those who listened to the proffers or menaces of the Persian.

Ægina was an island which of a flat and stoney soil, had from the very first necessitated its inhabitants to seek sustenance from the seas; the bark was soon improved into the vessel, the troop of fishermen became a nation of merchants, and its naval experience and power, during the usurpations at Athens, had arrogated the dominion of the seas.

The disgust of these too neighbouring rivals (for Ægina was within sight of Attica) was

easily

easily to be enflamed into a war; and the present demeanor of the islanders gave a pretext for hostility to the Athenians, the most optionable and glorious: the Æginetans being however subordinate to the Spartan, it was first thought proper to demand chastisement at the hands of the sovereign state—of the people who had acted in a manner derogatory to the honor of Greece, had spurned the compact of its associated cities, and abetted the designs of its enemies: the Spartans gave ear to the remonstrance, and taking ten of the chief citizens from Ægina, pledged them to Athens in security for the fidelity of their countrymen; these again quickly made reprisals on the coast of Attica, and after various altercation, a naval war broke out between Ægina and Athens, and was sometime carried on with various success, but with uniform animosity and exertion. This private contest merits our attention, as it marks the progress of, and has its share in accounting for the Athenian greatness at sea,——for those " *wooden walls*—which so suddenly rose up, the safeguard and bulwark of Greece: the expedition to the coast of Ionia, and attack of Sardis, had awakened the spirit of naval prowess; and the Æginetan war had taught the ship-

builder

builder and engineer, the advantages of their art; and given the mariner the courage and dexterity of habit.

Darius's forces to the amount of two hundred thousand foot, and ten thousand horse, were now mustered in Cilicia, and ready for embarkation: six hundred vessels of war were already hovering on the coasts, and this formidable armament taking aboard the troops, immediately pointed its course to Eubæa: the city of Eretria in that island, had likewise given some support to the insurgents of Ionia, and Datis the Persian general, was ordered by the king, to bring the whole of that and the Athenian people in chains to the foot of his throne.

This haughty mandate, and the mighty force destined to its accomplishment, intimidated the independant republics, and turned the attention of all from intestine broils, to the means of common safety: in vain however the islands boasted the parade of opposition, to so numerous an enemy; they were quickly over-run and despoiled; even Eretria made but a short resistance; and Datis having thus in part effected his commission, sent a multitude of every age and sex, to await the sentence of Darius: four thousand men whom Athens had generously af-
forded

forded in fuccour, were as generoufly difmiffed by the Eretrians, previous to the moment of defpair, that furrendered up their liberties; and they opportunely returned for the defence of their native country.——" The Perfian camp
" is pitched on the plains of Marathon, let us
" ——(faid Miltiades)—let us meet them with
" ardour in the field;——vain is the idea of
" fafety within thefe walls; impatience of con-
" finement, and the feelings of private attach-
" ment, and of private intereft, ever have,
" and will beget treachery; and fhould this not
" be the cafe, ftill the firft emotion of courage
" deadens, unlefs animated by the heat of en-
" terprize;—the fpirit of men lofes force in a di-
" vifion of pofts; embody your citizens, lead
" them undauntedly forth, and emulation and
" patriotifm will effect wonders."

The advice of Miltiades was adopted, and how juft the reafoning, and how provident of events, every after-circumftance will evince!——during the conflict at Marathon, (the particulars of which I think it inconfequential to recite) a fhield was by fome traitor-hand held up at Athens, in token to the Perfian fleet, that the walls were vacate; but the citizens returned in time from the completion of their victory,

victory, to fruſtrate the treachery, and repel the invaders.

The commonwealth began now to feel, and glory in, the effects of its happy eſtabliſhment; the firſt means of its liberty were recalled to mind, the firſt moment was ſanctified, the firſt authors venerated: the deed of Ariſtogeiton and Harmodius was again held up to public view; decree enſued decree in honor of their names; no ſlave was ever after to bear the ſame appellation; their martyrdom was conſigned to the chorus at the Panathanæan feſtival, and their ſtatues were anew cut out in braſs, and by the hand of Praxiteles.

The conduct and valour of Miltiades were crowned too with marks of public favor and renown: his portrait was painted at the head of the ten generals, who led forth the ten thouſand brave citizens of Athens, to the conqueſt of twenty times their number; and the hero was contented with his reward.

When pecuniary or other recompenſe of worldly value is beſtowed on a great or good deed, and the gift to virtue, is the ſame with the hire of vice; the diſtinction is much impaired, and the purity of the motive no longer being aſcertained, the action is no longer in

the

the same manner ennobled by its reward; the high minded then disdaining to receive in common with those of sordid views, the incentive of glory loses ground, and the hopes of payment enlarge their influence, till in fine the unworthy alone push forward to notice and retribution through means corrupting and destructive to the commonwealth: public virtue is then lost, and with it the republic.

The Persian forces were effectually repulsed, and had now retired homeward in dismay: seventy vessels were fitted out from Athens to scour the seas, and levy fines on such of the islands, as by apostacy to the common cause, or a neutral policy, had avoided the danger, and were now to reap the fruits of the victory. A contribution from these states was deemed a just demand, and Miltiades was sent at the head of the fleet, to command and enforce the impost. His first destination was to Paros, where by accident being frustrated of his purpose, and severely wounded too in the thigh, he returned successless and despirited to Athens. The people were astonished at the repulse! an Athenian armament, and under the conduct of Miltiades was to be irresistable! the leader surely must have betrayed the duties of his command, and

and have tampered with the Persian, or very islands he was sent to tax or punish! discontent often gives birth to general rumour, and rumour to particular suspicion: the conduct of Miltiades was arraigned and condemned, and a heavy fine imposed, from the weight of which, and of his country's displeasure, he was freed by a sudden death, the consequence of the wound got in its service.

Ingratitude is a topic on which the declaimer rivets the attention of his audience.——It touches home to the selfishness of benevolence; ——it paints an irksome picture of the interest generosity takes in expected retribution, and anger (from dissatisfaction of the conscience thus awakened to itself) irritates, and vexes the mind with the object that occasioned it; the motives of this involuntary anger we are not willing to sift to the bottom, but hastily attribute it to an antipathy of the vicious and the mean;——but the vicious and the mean start with horror at the same tale of benefit ill-repayed: the quality of their mite of goodness is equally dear, and the proof of the alloy, equally distressful: It must be this facility of awakening emotion, and interesting the reader, or self-deception, or misapplication of the term, that

hath

hath betrayed so many writers into the absurdity of harranguing on the ingratitude of a collected state to a subject thereof.——Hath not the sensible Feyjo in his Theatros Criticos, and the Florentine in his discourses, and Stanyan in his history, and all the Belles-Lettres-writers of the French,——have they not twitted the Athenians with ingratitude to private citizens?——as if, in any vicious sense, (and in any other sense, I think the word hath no meaning) a republic could be ungrateful to a constituent!

It is a mark of general depravity, when adulation exalts the mere duties of life: a just idea of what we owe to our country, precludes all works of superorogation in the pure faith of patriotism, as in that of religion: when we have done all we can, we have done but what we ought; in the lesser as in the more general system we should with resignation often consider a private evil as the public benefit; and look on the *" *vox populi*, if not that of God,

---

* Et non senza cagione si assomiglia la voce d'un populo a quello d'Iddio, perche si vede una opinione universale, fare affetti meravigliosi ne' pronostichi suoi; tal che pare che per occulta virtu, prevegga il suo male, et il suo bene.

Machiavele in L. 1mo. de discorsi, cap. 58.

God, yet as worthy to be held in secondary veneration. Each citizen that assembled for the ostracism or other mode of judicature, met to consider of the safety and weal of the republic; from the moment he was in his public capacity, no other than public views were to influence his vote; it was not whether the man proceeded against, had hitherto been of service, but whether in future he might be of diservice to the state; he was to consider himself as an advocate retained on the part of his country, that its safety and well-being now and hereafter depended on his voice, and that it was not justifiable to reject the merest surmise of danger to many, in favor to one; no lustre of private character was to dazzle, and draw his attention from the common weal; if a thought of the man intruded, it was derogatory to the duty of the citizen:———" Miltiades behaved " justly in the Chersonese;———*true, but he* " *there assumed the ensigns and honors of a* " *king:*"—His manners are plausible, his eloquence popular, his valour approved;—" *it* " *was the very character of Pisistratus:*"—Remember the victory at Marathon;—" *doth not* " *himself remember it too much?*"—His enmity with the Persian king, must surely be irreconcileable,

cileable, for could Darius forget the hardy proposal made on the banks of the Danube?—" *Aye, but when Tissaphernes sent stores to Attica, it was on the intercession, and to the faith of* Miltiades alone, *that he would trust them:*"——says Nepos—*Hæc populus respiciens malluit eum innoxium plecti, quàm se diutius esse in timore.*

CHAP.

CHAP. XII.

DARIUS irritated by the defeat, was gathering together the fugitives from Marathon, levying new forces, building ships, every way preparing a vast armament to crush and extirpate the very name of Athens,—when death stept in between—and put a sudden stop to his career of vanity, rage, and folly.

A young and ignorant youth upon the throne; a minister sacrificing truth, honor, and the weal of thousands to a private purpose; that purpose effected by the foulest adulation; and that adulation opposed in vain, and with danger too, to the honest dissentient—a scene now become common place on the great theatre of the world, was then played in the council chamber of Persia: Xerxes opens the debate with much ignorance, and much arrogance; Mardonius prevails himself of the one, and flatters the other;—the speech of Artabanus I cannot so lightly pass over:—" Give some attention
" (said

" (said he) O king, to contrary counsel; the
" value of the previous opinion will then have
" some test; the sound quality of advice is to
" be ascertained by opposition alone:—where
" is this prowess that the Greeks are to find so
" irresistable?—Failed it not in Scythia?—
" Failed it not in Attica?—How few intrepid
" men there braved the assault of thousands?
" ——How fully did they evince that courage
" and unanimity could conquer in despight of
" multitudes!—and this bridge over the Helle-
" spont!—is it so soon then forgot, how nearly
" Darius and all the flower of Persia were be-
" trayed, and left victims to the colds and
" dearth of Scythia?—I shudder at the thought
" that the fate of our king, our all, depended
" on a single voice,—and that too of Histiæus,
" *the traitor!* but supposing this armament,
" this mighty fleet, these numerous troops, to
" be invincible;——can they subdue too the
" elements?—Your bridge, and your ships,
" may they not be shattered by storms? Or is
" armour proof against pestilence or famine?
" It is not the force of myriads that can oppose
" the will of heaven; as its thunders spare the
" lowly object, and beat down the oak or pa-
" lace; so God delights in abasing the arro-
                                    " gance

" gance of human wishes, and depresses the
" mightier and elevates the weaker power!—for
" know, O King, that *God jealous of the sentiment*
" *self-greatness, permitteth it but to himself alone!*"
—This speech (which I have closely copied from Herodotus) was received with contempt, and answered with passion; the speaker was called coward and dotard, and the expedition was resolved on: the debate then closed, the curtain dropt, and (according to the known inversion of the political theatre)——the farce being ended, the tragedy was to begin.

Let us pass over the musters and march of the army, and hasten to fix Xerxes and the Persian camp near Tempe in Thessaly. The storm rumbled from afar, and Greece awakened to the sound! a common senate was called, every private pretension and contest was waved, levies were ordered, taxes imposed, alliances suggested, and every means of defence explored, argued, and expedited. Synætus the Spartan, and Themistocles were immediately sent forward with ten thousand men to meet the Persian, to solicit adherence to the common cause, to fix the wavering, to attach he dissentient; and every where collecting what troops they could, to harrass the invaders, and cutting off their provisions and forage to retard their progress, and give the Grecian council time to think, and act best for the common security. These generals were in many parts frustrated of success;—some states were alienated by disgust, the generous wishes of some were repressed by inability or fear, and others motiv'd by lucre deigned not even to plead present ease or danger, but openly abetted the designs of the enemy. The emissaries dispatched in quest of succour from Apulia and Sicily met not with a more favourable reception: the Carthaginians intimidated by the vicinity of Ægypt, (then a a province of the Persian empire) had entered into an offensive alliance with Xerxes, and the part assigned them, was to keep the Greek settlements in Italy, and Sicily too fully employed, to any ways afford assistance to the mother-country. Under these accumulated distresses and disappointments, it was judged expedient to study every means of protracting the war, and heaven in default of other allies, might perhaps abet so just a cause, and with defease tempest or famine, vex and diminish their enemies. Leonidas and the Spartans undertook to retard for sometime the Persian inroad into Greece; and it is well known how resolutely at Thermopylæ those brave

brave troops effected the purpose, and bartered their lives for the safety of their country.

In the war with Darius we saw the Athenians firmly dispute the field of battle, we saw the unanimity of patriots substitute to the discipline of soldiers, produce as combined and as irresistable a force; we are now to view them in a different scene of action—to behold them driven vagabon'd to the seas, and in this their distress, opening another sluice, and rushing in a new channel to honor and dominion!

The confederate fleet was stationed near Artemisium in Eubæa; the Persian admiral sent round three hundred vessels to block up this armament in the narrow strait that divides that island from the continent, and intercept them in retreat; this haughty indication of superiority awakened the indignation of the Greeks, and that and despair of flight urged them to await the conflict with the sullen resolution of those who foresee, and are prepared for the worst.

Though the Athenians, from regard to the common union waved all pretensions to the supreme command, yet Eurybiades the Spartan leader in every case of difficulty recurred to the genius of Themistocles;—This Athenian was endowed with a larger portion of etherial spirit

than

than in the munificence of nature is often allotted to one man;—daring in enterprize, cool in action, of a foresight like prophecy, a comprehension intuitive, and a memory (as himself declared) retentive even to a pain, was this extraordinary character,—and it quickly gained an ascendancy which no political arrangement could preclude;—was the commander of Sparta, of Tegeæa, or Ægina, or ought other state, still to Themistocles every mind looked up for scheme, every eye for example: he perceived that the spirit of his countrymen deadened in inaction; he well knew that defence was of a sluggish cast, that attack anticipated the air of triumph, and he accordingly used every art to persuade them to provoke the combat, and go forth and assail the Persian detachment: he succeeded; and the conflict though not decisive, gave the allied Greeks better hopes of victory;—It show'd that valour had its superiority as well as multitude, and taught them for the future to regard disparity of force, as distinct from that of numbers.

Xerxes and his army were now far in their way to Attica, the country was depopulated, the city defenceless—" shall we then forsake our " ships?—no (said Themistocles)—rather let us " use them to save our wives, our children, our
" all

"all that is dear to us:—grieve not at the battering of your walls;—the republic lives not in its edifices but its men; not the city, but the citizens make the state;—save them, and Athens is still great, and may yet be happy." This desperate resource was adopted, and those, whom sex, decrepitude, or infancy rendered unfit for service, were deposited in Salamis, Ægina, and other neighbouring islands, to await better times for their restoration to their native gods and country.

In the chain of affection, patriotism appears a necessary link intermediate to social love, and general philanthrophy:—the man who loves not his country, can be no very warm friend to mankind: thus we find the Athenians showed more ardour for, and more benevolence to the common cause than any other of the Greeks; the Spartans indeed were equally attached to their Sparta, but not equally to the common welfare; to account for this exception we must observe, that institution with them supplaced nature with habit, that habit transcends not its practice, and that their devotion was thus bounded by the maxims and exercise of duty prescribed to the narrow circle of their own state.

Much

Much as Athens had suffered, and constant as she was in her sufferings, the other allies were little willing to risque any thing for her support or consolation: a selfish system of conduct was adopted, the fortification of the isthmus, and the station of the fleet on the coasts of the Peloponnese were determined on by the confederates whose possessions lay in those parts: Themistocles saw the danger of this narrow policy, that the different detachments quitting the general rendezvous were likely to quit the common cause; some would retire to their native harbours, some sell their freedom, and some seek it on a distant and unmolested shore;—and were the Athenian wives and daughters to be left defenceless, and devoted to all the outrage of captivity?—were the people to be forsaken, who had forsaken their all to preserve their faith, and take so hardy a part in the perils too of others?—Some of the Greeks went so far as to reject the Athenian voice in council, to cavil at their very existence as a state, and basely twit them with the loss of that country, they had given up from such public-spirited and noble motives: incensed at the insult, the Athenians declared,—They still had, and should soon display, their consequence;—that they would depart for Siris

in

in Italy, the propitious spot of settlement pointed out to them by the oracle; and the Peloponnesians would then feel how much they had lost, and severely rue the insolence of their present deportment. This menace caused at least some hesitation, and Themistocles prevailed himself of the moment of delay to frustrate the scheme of retreat and force an engagement: he found means of informing Xerxes of the intended departure, and with specious argument, and under the mask of treasonable friendship, persuaded him to intercept the pass, and attack the Grecians when in the disorder and dismay of flight; the stratagem succeeded, the Persian fleet blocked up the road; and Themistocles then aprizing the confederates of the impracticability of escape, necessity held the place of virtue, and they pre-prepared for the combat.

On one side behold the naval force of half the known world, and amidst a croud of uncouth names and barbarous novelties, discover too the most experienced and renown'd of maritime nations,—the veteran sailors of the isles, of the Euxine sea and of Ægypt;—remark too three hundred vessels from Sidonia and Syria, and manned by those Phænicians whose prowess and practice are the favourite themes of antiquity!

On

On the other part, view the armament of the Greeks;—a small but desperate band, not equalling in numbers the twentieth part of the enemy, but still placing a forlorn hope of victory in the resolution to die for it!

Themistocles studied every means to lessen or baffle the superiority of the enemy: he tampered with the Asiatic Greeks, and making them, or making them seem, inclinable to desert, rendered them suspicious to the king, and they were not permitted to mingle in the combat: he artfully contrived to draw the Persian into the narrow seas, where the previous orders and arrangements of so crouded a fleet were impeded and broken, and in the moment of embarrassment he gave the signal for attack; the Greeks rushed with impetuosity into the midst of the enemy, sunk some vessels, disordered the whole body, forced many on shore, and many finding their very efforts to engage fruitless, withdrew from the scene of action: to particularize a modern battle may perhaps please some military reader; but I see little instruction and much pedantry in the detail of ancient warfare; let us then conclude the fight of Salamis, and say, victory was decisive on the part of the Greeks. Though many ships were sunk and many stranded, yet it

was

was to be supposed that of so vast a fleet sufficient might remain to be still formidable, and bring the superiority at sea again to hostile discussion.—Justin clears up this difficulty with observing, that those who had escaped or avoided the conflict, dreading the resentment and cruelty of the king as much, or more than even the bravery of the foe, slunk off in secrecy to their respective ports and cities.

Arrogance and meanness of spirit belong to dirt of the same mold!—this Xerxes—this haughty Lord of half mankind, dismayed by a single defeat, flies towards the Hellespont, fearful lest his bridge should be broken down, a retreat cut off, and three millions of soldiers be necessitated to cope with a few petty and exhausted republics! He left however Mardonius to carry on the war, or rather (as I think Diodorus of Sicily hints) to cover his retreat; for the army was not deemed adequate to the prior purpose, and Mardonius retired northward to recruit, and add to his forces.

The threat of secession from the league dropt by the Athenians previous to the fight, was not readily forgot; whatever provocation called forth the menace, the menace alone was remembered,

and

and with all the bitterness of disgust, for hatred often finds new subject in its very injustice.

When Eurybiades was to bestow the palm of virtue, he passed by the Athenians, and gave to their rivals the Æginetans the first place of desert: the Spartans however feared the abilities of Themistocles, and while they insulted the people, to conciliate their general, loaded him with presents and applause: the Athenians were too high-minded to stoop to reproach or complaint; but their indignation vented itself on Themistocles, who had held his hand forth for the gift, and from a mercenary consideration, had waved the memory of the many indignities offered to his country: he was immediately degraded, and the command given to Xantippus. Attica was now vacated by the Persian, and affection for the natal soil——that endearment which the recollection of tender or happy incidents gives to the scene of past enjoyment (deemed enjoyment perhaps because past)——and a superstitious veneration of some spots, and the attachment use gives to all, urged the fugitives to immediately reclaim the site of their native city, repair its ruins, rebuild its walls, and propitiate its gods with new sacrifices and temples.

The

The restless ambition of Themistocles ill-brooked the disgrace he was under with his fellow-citizens; and to recover their favor, his genius agitated every plan of private artifice, or of public service: convening the assembly, in a bold and artful harrangue, he hinted at a scheme of the utmost importance to the state, but which notoriety would frustrate the execution of;—he therefore demanded the assistance of such good and wise citizens as could be relied on by the community: singly, Aristides was judged to be of wisdom and integrity adequate to the trust, and he was commanded to attend to, and report his opinion of the project in view. Aristides on a future day stept forth, and without preamble of approbation or dislike, merely declared that the scheme was equally replete with benefit to themselves, and with injustice to others; and without further enquiry it was unanimously rejected.

The very essence of a popular government (says Montesquieu) is virtue;—it is indeed the soul of a republic, and dissolution attends its exit: Dynasties may stand on a basis of various substance, of force of institution, or mere prescription; but a democracy requires the precious

cious cement of probity fifted from every particle of vicious or felfish inclination: the ftate cannot long exift but of good citizens, and the good citizen hath its foundation in the good man;—patriotifm may be termed an alchemy elaborated of all private virtues: obferve well, that had Athens paid the lighteft attention to the policy of Themiftocles, it muft have been from felfish views, and every citizen who had given a voice even for the debate, muft have been actuated by motives that marked him as a member dangerous to the future commonweal.

The Athenians of all others were moft the object of dread to the common enemy; Marathon echoed the hiftory of their valour, Salamis of their policy; and the force accruing to the confederacy from their peculiar vigour and credit was obvious on repeated trial: Mardonius pondered how to detach this people from the alliance; their patrimonies were plundered, and themfelves and families doomed to a long and laborious penury; mifery might at length perhaps have broken the firmnefs of their fpirit, and have alienated their minds from fo diftreffful a caufe: (to ufe the elegant words of Tacitus)

citus)——*certamen virtutis et ambitio gloriæ felicium hominum funt affectus!*

Minifters were difpatched to Athens with every threat that could influence, and every proffer that might feduce;—would they pay a titular hommage, and be merely nominal tributaries to Xerxes, the faireft fpot of Greece, or of the known world was at their choice; their city fhould be rebuilt, and public edifices erected and endowed with fplendor and with opulence; nor fhould a law be touched, or privilege be invaded: the Spartans fent emiffaries in hafte and terror to meet and oppofe this embaffy; they were confcious of the ill-treatment which Athens might plead in vindication of infidelity to the Grecian league, and they came ready fraught with argument, entreaty and reproach.

On this occafion, there was a dignity in the conduct of the Athenian fenate which never can fufficiently be admired: the propofals of Mardonius were received with a contemptuous filence;—the ambaffadors fimply were defired to immediately quit the city; for the fenate revered the facred character, and was unwilling it fhould meet with the infult, any delay within thofe walls might expofe it to:—to the Spartans they replied

plied in the haughty tone of offended defert, and bad them for the future judge better of their virtue and their fervices.

Mardonius exafperated at the repulfe, again poured his myriads into Attica, and again the aged and the weak were wafted to the neighbouring coafts, and the city deftroyed, and its very foundations erafed. As if their country was endeared by adverfity, the people this time lingered to the laft moment within their town, nor quitted it, till their fupplications for reinforcement had been rejected by Sparta, and every other city of the league. It foon appeared that an engagement though procraftinated, could not be avoided; Mardonius advanced raging with fire and fword from territory to territory, and then at length the cogency of their own affairs induced the Peloponnefians to take the field, and the confederate army as foon as collected, advanced to meet the enemy, then defolating the plains of Platæa. Paufanias the Spartan king commanded the allied forces confifting of an hundred thoufand combatants;—a number by far greater than the Grecians had ever heretofore muftered in one field of battle. Let us not dwell on inconfequent particulars;—the victory

tory at Platæa though more sharply contested, was again decisive in favour of the Greeks;—the Persian generals were killed, the whole army routed, and the carnage pursued with such rage and animosity, that fortunate was the Persian who escaped to tell his king,—how prophetic were the tears he shed, when numbering his millions at Sardis!

Leutychides and Xantippus still pursuing and harrassing the remains of the fleet worsted at Salamis, at length forced it from the seas;—the mariners no longer daring to face the naval power of the Greeks, drew their vessels on shore, and by a fortification and entrenchment, sought to secure them from the enemy; but nothing could stop the ardour of conquest;—the Grecians sallied from their ships;—impediment and numbers were slighted;—nothing could resist the confidence and strength of the assailants; and the very day that crowned the Greeks with victory at Platæa, gave them the laurel too at Mycale.

The mighty armament employed on this expedition, was the united effort of the vast empire of Persia, and its forces being thus successively worsted, and its fleets destroyed, Xerxes was no longer in capacity of carrying hoftilities abroad, but embittered with difappointed vanity, was left to vent its cruelty on his fubjects, or bury its poignancy in diffipation, till vice and tyranny exceeded even the bounds of Afiatic fufferance, and he fell a victim to the public refentment.

CHAP.

CHAP. XIII.

OFtentimes a rational enquiry proves introductory to the emotions of the heart, and gives birth to a pleasure the more strong, as proceeding from the united impulse of argument and passion; whilst we trace the vicissitudes of human lot; whilst we study to obviate our own or others frailties; whilst we glean knowledge and happiness from the fields of error and misfortune,—we become interested in the characters of our lesson, a generous sympathy mixes itself with our speculations, and as reason approves or condemns every nerve vibrates in harmony to the sentiment: we become censors with Cato, and patriots with Brutus, and for a moment enter into the habitudes of the society artfully introduced to us by the writer, as strongly as those of our daily and domestic intercourse. The facility of particular applications, and the interest therein taken by the generality of readers, have induced many historians to make public events secondary to private characters; and instead of attempting to absorb the attention in the weal and fortunes of the collected state, to take the easier task of painting a single life, and attaching the student by the refined flattery of raising in him ascititious feelings, and then placing them in a proud self-comparison with the picture. Even those who give the most idle perusal to a work, are yet from daily practice habituated to a consideration of the virtues and vices of an individual, but when the actions of a combined society are in view, the lengthened chain requires the most assiduous spirit to unravel it, much penetration to discover the minute links, and much acuteness to scrutinize their multiplicate relations and dependencies.

More are capable of feeling than of speculating; perhaps all men are fonder of sentiment than thought; and when I presume to blame those who have turned history into adventure, and have emulated the portrait-painter, whose colossal heroe stalks in front of a town or a battle scarcely the dimension of his shoe,—when I propose every where to elevate the battle and the town,——to take virtue, as much as may be, in the aggregate, nor depress the characteristic of a people by an unnatural and degrading

contrast

contrast with the character of one man, perhaps I may afford less entertainment than those I am bold to censure; but my first end in penning this historical essay, is during a retirement and vacancy of employ, ill-suited to the activity of my temper, to write something for self-exercise and improvement, and success as an author is but a secondary view.

Great men I am apt to look upon as factitious beings; the further the analysis is pursued, the more rational the *nil admirari* of the old Numicus will appear;——the more we shall be led to think that they are much indebted to casualties for their elevation; and remarking the extravagancies on which their pretensions to superiority are often founded, perhaps imagine that merit as well as opulence, are in the hands of fortune; whilst by her good favor crimes are aggrandized into heroism, and vice which in a meaner state was turned from with abhorrence, becomes respected in its excess. Even the real virtue which some few times hath found its way to preheminence, perhaps was not of a more sublimate or etherial temper, than that of myriads depressed in oblivion; as the statue of Memnon in Ægypt, which spoke when the rising sun beam'd on its head, so

many

many a seeming block in private life might vivify, were a timely ray of fortune directed to its recefs of spirit : perhaps those minds endowed with the most transcendant qualities, have through every age passed with little notice, or even esteem;——the soldier who asked Miltiades wherefore he wore the laurel his country had won (if he spoke not from envy) was of more intrinsic worth than Miltiades : some alloy is necessary to make a character current: the younger Pliny well observes,—" that genius cannot alone struggle into day; it must be drawn forth by season and circumstance, nor will this suffice, unless too it be abetted by the patronage of social favor and introduction."——Is there a man so visionary and so little practiced in life, as not to know, that the price of public notice is the abasement of many parts necessary to the theory of exalted virtue? The candidate must often prostitute his opinion, if not his morals ; it is the only key to the barrier of vanity, and if he disdain that path to the good graces of mankind, he had better foregoe all hopes of attainment; and after all, and even the most brilliant exertion of ability, the simple reason of preference will often prevail, which raised Poppæus Sabinus to the favor of the

emperor.

emperor Claudius—*nullam ob eximiam artem, sed quod par negotiis neque supra erat:* a policy well deserving attention.

The subtilty of intellect, or spirit of entreprize, or what else may enter into the composition of those we vulgarly term "Great men, are particularly to be guarded against in popular governments: ascendency of private character may discompose the union or corrupt the virtue of the people; favour to particular men may beget factions in the state, and social love recoil from the extent of patriotism, to the narrow circle of a party; then is it retreated midway to domestic and to self-interest;—self-interest in its turn will quickly sway, and the whole commonwealth be distracted with various and private influences.

Even a virtuous man too much distinguished and exalted above his peers may open this sluice to the ruin of his country: let us draw a character more dangerous, and more fitted for self-elevation,—let us delineate the hero of Salamis:

——" His mind was of a sublimate and active spirit, that pervaded in a momentary course, the past, the present and the future; and had a command of experience, subtilty, and foresight for the exigencies of the hour, as for the protractions of policy; quick in thought, and tardy to execute;

cute; or dilatory in purpose, and immediate and bold in perpetration, as juncture necessitated, or as season required: no scheme was too deep for his capacity; no enterprize too hardy for his courage; he had not the winning softness, but he had the force of eloquence; his tongue was not persuasive but commanding;—its art was the simplicity of truth; when he spoke, it was not a plausibility of address, it was not a specious display of argument, or an appeal to the pathetic that drew the favour of the assembly, but a something comprehensive, intuitive, prophetic,—a something of genius that rivetted the attention, and on the self-diffidence of the hearer raised an uncontrolable command; the minds of the audience were amazed and daunted into acquiescence, even when not argued into conviction; and the artful rhetor forgot his art, and the opinionative were abashed before him!— Such or like preheminence of character was fatal to the commonwealth of Athens: Miltiades prepared the way for Themistocles; Themistocles for Pericles; crouching to the successive ascendancy of their great men, the people were habitually brought to consider their popular state as dependant; and rather confide their public weal to the abilities of a statesman, than to the wisdom of the

constitution;

constitution: they insensibly deviated from the sound and simple principle of conduct adopted by their forefathers, and to a free progress in the strait road of virtue, prefer'd a leading string in the maze of politics; they were then often led to injustice, often bewildered in ruinous practices, often betrayed to bloody and useless expeditions; at length enured to subserviency they were at times the means of glory and power to the ambitious, tools to the crafty, wealth to the avaricious, and a subterfuge to the criminal; when the farce of their sanction was not needed, they were allured from the Forum to the Piræeus, of citizens were made mere merchants, and taught a lesson of lucre and dissipation that encreased their disrelish for public duties, and threw further opportunity of malverfation into the hands of their demagogue: an assembly of citizens, after the time of Pericles could rarely be formed, but by bribes to the alert, and fines on those of tardy appearance:—*an office was instituted for that purpose alone.*

The people of Athens reclaiming their native soil planned their new city on a larger, and improved scale; the old port Phaleron seemed of too small extent, and the foundations of a more commodious receptacle for their shipping were

now

now laid at the Piræeus ; an arſenal and ſpacious inercantile key were deſigned, and were to be ſurrounded with walls of an extraordinary height, and of a thickneſs that would admit two chariots to paſs on the ſummit ; and the ſtones were to be rivetted with iron, and cemented with molten lead : The Spartans viewed with jealouſy and fear the progreſs of theſe mighty works ; they remonſtrated againſt the policy of ſuch fortification—" might it not prove a place of arms for the Perſian !"—againſt the injuſtice of it ;—" why diſtruſt their friends and allies ?"—The Athenians anſwered not with their old-faſhioned noble ſincerity ;—they truſted not to a fair parley, or to a brave defiance ;—remark very particularly their conduct (even Juſtin the epitomiſt has particularly remarked it)—They were perſuaded *by their great man*—to trick, to evade, to trifle—to ſay and to unſay,—and to prefer a low craftyhood to an honeſt appeal to the juſtice of the allies, or to a reliance on their own force : Themiſtocles in the ſiniſter means he took of rebuilding and ſtrengthening Athens, more effectually ſerved the dominion of Sparta by corrupting the people, than he annoyed it by fortifying the city : this was the firſt blow given to public virtue,—the commonwealth ſhook to its very foundation,

dation, and a crevice was ever after open to matter of corrosive sap, or of sudden explosion.

The expedition of Xerxes though successless to the invader, was not the less fatal to Greece; the profusion of gold and silver found in the Persian camp after the battle of Platæa, and the inundation of wealth poured into the country from the several other victories, anticipated greatly the progress of particular accumulation, and of general luxury; private citizens became distinguished, and soon distinguishable alone, by their superior opulence: Cimon, whose patrimony, we are told, was insufficient to pay his father's debt to the public, suddenly became possessed of so great wealth, that feasting the commonalty of Athens was with him an ordinary expence.

The redemption of the captives too returned a prodigious sum to the conquerors; and the multitude who were not ransomed, taking the menial trades and services from the citizens, taught them (as we shall duly observe) a fatal lesson of pride and overbearance. Other slaves were sent to the silver mines in Attica, which although (according to Xenophon) worked from time immemorial had hitherto been productive of a scanty revenue, but were now likely to be labored with

a toil-a toilsome assiduity that promised the most abundant returns.—So many springs of corruption at once burst the sod!—the sluices they tore up,—the stoppages they bore away, and channels they pursued, shall be delineated in their proper chart.

Succesful in her defence, Greece in her turn brandished the hostile sword, and in the arrogance of triumph meditated new victories in the very heart of Asia. Many of the Greek colonies had come over during the contest, all were lukewarm to the Persian cause, and had proved rather an encumbrance, than support, to the armaments they were inlisted into: to protect these people and save them from the vengeance of Xerxes was the ostensible, and indeed a just reason for still protracting the war;—but the avidity of glory as of wealth encreases with acquisition, and motives of ambition and avarice probably lurked beneath the semblance of disinterested bravery and beneficence.

The Spartans still kept the lead in the confederacy, Pausanias their king was still vested with the supreme command, and still the allies collectively submitted to a military jurisdiction.

The education of the Lacedæmonian youth pretended not to teach them, but to confine them

them to the best road;—to fix them in a singular walk of virtue guarded by dæmons and bugbears, wherein they were goaded on by shame and pride, and frighten'd with whips and masks on the minutest tendency to linger or to deviate, till in fine habit hardened or conciliated their minds to the rugged way. This institution however so much outraged nature, and so much infringed her original claims to various temperature of passion and of mind, that the legislator forsaw she must ever be on the watch to assert her rights, and invalidate his system: it was therefore his policy to have as little inroad to her as possible, and to cut off all connexion with those whose example might too amiably enforce her interests and cause: He permitted no strangers to sojourn in his city, or citizens to travel into strange countries; even war too often waged with the same people was proscribed as being too familiar and corruptive an intercourse; (the apprehension of teaching the enemy I think falsely attributed as his motive, for the Spartans knew less of the *art* of war, than any of the Greeks). Indeed in bounty to mankind Lycurgus having adopted such a scheme of government could not do less than study its immaculate continuance, for having treated men as

wild

wild beasts he had made them so; his plan was to chain and not to humanize, and the loosening of the fetter might be equally fatal to his people and to their neighbours.

The duration and commerce of the Persian war had served much to relax the Spartan severity, and having foregone the strict spirit of their discipline, they had no just theory of ethics whence to medicate the ill, and they rushed headlong into every kind of barbarous insolence and unpolished debauchery.

The allies beheld the conduct of Pausanias and his followers with indignation, and one by one they withdrew from his command and submitted themselves to the generalship of Cymon and Aristides: the Ephori saw their institution in danger, and waving for the present all other considerations sullenly acquiesced in the supremacy of Athens.

A fixed establishment of proportional subsidies was a necessary measure previous to any new expedition: each state accordingly consented to an assessment at such rates of men and monies, as the general exigency and its respective strength might authorise; and the Athenians were permitted to commence their administration with assuming the important authority of fixing, collecting,

lecting, and managing the quota of each member-city of the confederacy: this truft, we are told, was executed by Ariftides with a ftrict faith and impartiality that gave new afcendency to him and to his country; but the courfe of fuch power was corruptive and ruinous; and the diveftment thereof difficult, as the continuance dangerous.

The ill-policy indeed of confiding the fole conduct of the levies to any fingle ftate feems fo very obvious, that a curious reader might requeft a nicer fearch into this fingular matter: it will be obferved, (as it indeed prov'd) that a power thus repofed, indefinite in extent as in duration, was virtually perpetual and defpotic; for could the period of its authority be queftioned, whilft that authority was in full force;—or its force be fafely excepted to, when its expiation was not at hand;—fubmiffion to fuch a command was in time likely to fall into fervitude, and diffention at all times to bear the mein of hoftility: It was probable that the party repofed in progreffively would admit the fole alternative of conftant fervice or virulent enmity. Confidering the facility of obviating fo fatal confequences by the fimple eftablifhment of a council or committee of the feveral ftates, it is difficult

ficult to account for their coinciding in so destructive a measure: perhaps dazzled by a successive and rapid course of conquest, they gave not leisure to political consideration, but blindly adopted what seemed readiest for the present purpose, and made choice of a sole and uncontrolable command as best fitted for war,—not provident that its consequences might extend to times of peace.

From this period the conduct of the Athenians at home and abroad wore a new aspect, was founded on new principles of government, and model'd to a new system of politics; their future career therefore shall be reserved for disquisition in another book.

The completion of the war with Persia was hereafter involved with a series of local interests and intestine commotions; so far however it may be proper to anticipate events, as not to leave the reader in any incertitude with respect to a conclusion of hostilities with the common enemy:—this thread of history indeed runs but lightly through the web, which simply spotted with the victories over the Persian at Cyprus and Eurymedon is every where interwoven with the varieties of national party, usurpation and quarrel;

rel;—the victories at Eurymedon and Cyprus closed the contest with Xerxes, and a peace was concluded in terms the most glorious and beneficial to Greece and her allies, and the most humiliating to their aggressor.

K   BOOK

BOOK THE SECOND.

CHAP. I.

WHERE is happiness to be found? the man of power who shines the sun of his little sphere, whose every nod is obey'd, and every folly flattered, still restless and ill-contented, pushes forward to new schemes of happiness, and risques his all in pursuit of some untasted acquisition: The wealthy, whose every wish is anticipated by gratification, seems not more blest in his peculiar lot, but peevishly complains of satiety, and listens with attention to the visionary talker of woods and rocks, and the felicity of a rural solitude:——ask the hermit—if retirement can give the promised bliss?—from pride he will perhaps affirm so;—but in terms of misanthropy and discontent which surely evince the folly of the assertion!

Happiness is no where to be found, but every where to be sought for.

The huntsman lays his account of pleasure not in the capture, but in the chace of the game;—so the greater objects of human attachment interest in the pursuit, and soon give difrelish in the tranquillity of the possession.——The elastic æther which flows in the channels of the nerves, and inspirits the mass of the brain, requires motion and expenditure, not to stagnate in torpid compressure, load the blood, and thicken the humours, 'till the habit is replete with horrors and with melancholy.

Divinely is it thus instituted, that the activity of our faculties should constitute our happiness, whilst what blesses the individual, enriches the species; and the pursuit which gives pleasure to each, tends to some acquisition productive of further distinctions to humanity, and elevating it more and more, in the system of which it makes a part.

From motion comes enjoyment;--hence the rich man would be richer, the great man greater; and all would add to, or change something, to-morrow, of what they possess to-day :—hence the despot would still subject one province more ;—the tear of Alexander, that there were no more worlds to conquer, belongs to every human eye in the private circle of difficulties surmounted or subdued ; the final conquest is pleasureable only in expectation ;—to the harrassed veteran it may indeed

be

be optionable,---but to provoke rest in the brightness of the day, is to expose the impatient mind to uneasy sleeps and painful dreams.

Sylla enjoyed the energy of contention, but found the object thereof not worth retaining; and Cæsar, long harrassed by foreign wars, and newly escaped from civil broils, perceived ease to be incompatible with his happiness, and at the hour of his death was meditating on the extremes of Parthia as new scenes of conquest, and a new means of felicity, to result from the ardour of his spirit. Why are we tenacious of liberty but because it gives an open field to that exertion of our minds or bodies, whence alone pleasure can proceed?——whether they are employed in tracking a wild beast, or in exploring a system, it is the same pleasure; and restriction to the man who hath once tasted it, is surely worse than death!

The discontented spirit of mankind, so often and so much deprecated by every trifler in metaphysics, is then found to be consistent with their happiness, and necessary to their improvement; nor is the mental inquietude of all, or particular ambition of the great, fit subject of contempt to the sage, or of wonder to the illiterate!

Is.

Is the reader yet aprized of the recondite principle of that ardour for acquisition, which impels an individual to gain, or a state to conquer?———Perceives he that it originates from an instinct rooted in our very nature, for wise and profitable ends?———Or without recurring to more remote, or more complicated reasoning; sees he not whence the Athenians, tranquil and undisturb'd at home, were actuated to the continuance of a war in search of power and dominion, the very success of which might be pronounced subversive of their commonwealth?

A republican government is replete with seeds of dissolution, some of speedy, some of slower growth, and all co-operating to a change of the constitution or ruin of the country.

The restless spirit above described, urging each to that exertion whence his happiness is to flow, will, under a monarchic, or the controul of other restrictive governments, of necessity expend itself in art or science, or in something, which without molestation of any, may turn to the account of all; but in a free state each individual, having some share in the political concern, may, perhaps, prefer that peculiar field of exercise to his mind, and progressively may, in his

active

active courſe, overleap the bounds of perſcriptive order, and ſafe adminiſtration. In a monarchy every ſituation is open but one; the viſionary may purſue honors, with as little detriment to the community, as the merchant his trade; or man of learning, ſcience; or the man of genius, art; but in a commonwealth a particular ſite is allotted to each, and the general arrangement is endangered, when any would deviate from their fixed place, in queſt of conſideration or aſcendancy. It is only in times of commotion, or by commotion, that at any rate this deſire of diſtinction can effect its purpoſe; and thence in the great book of experience we find the hiſtories of a republican people more particularly marked by epochs of inteſtine tumult and foreign war. From the moment conqueſt is the object of its policy, the exiſtence of the commonwealth is coeval only with the courſe of its victories; nor ultimately is its failure in arms leſs ruinous than its ſucceſs.—Grant that it conquer without loſs of people or diminution of funds;—ſuppoſe that the generals are actuated by none but public ambition, and that they reſume their private occupation, and rank without murmur, and without party;—ſuppoſe every favorable circumſtance even to a paradox;

paradox;—the succefsful war has added some city or some province, and will not such accession be the ruin of the capitol?—(I will again wave the fatal course of luxurious pride concomitant to national felicity;—I will confine my reasoning to the peculiarities of a democratic command) this city, this province,—how is it to be governed?———*Quid aliud* (says Tacitus) *exitio Athenienfibus fuit, quanquam armis pollerent, nisi quod subjectos pro alienigenis arcerent?*———But the contrary policy, were it not equally destructive?———Give the conquered people the rights of denizons;—let them in their respective cities, partake the free constitution of the democracy;—with the form of government will they not imbibe the high spirit and force which distinguish the donors?———Will they not as they favour liberty, disrelish command?——— the tree by natural growth raised above the shrub that sheltered its tender and first shoots, will it not crush it with the exuberance of its branches, exhaust its sources, and poison its head?——— The wary politician would in answer observe, that a contrary demeanor were of equally destructive tendency: a coercive and absolute command over a province annexed to the dominion of

a

a free state, must make a contract productive of discontent and every ill consequence hinted at in the words of the historian; what was gained by armies must be retained by similar means, and in times of trouble will be found not an accession to, but an incumbrance on, the republic; add,---that citizens of the superior state entrusted with a command foreign to the spirit of their own constitution will grow tainted by the examples of subserviency and habitudes of power; and return to corrupt the principles of their countrymen, and innovate on the commonwealth.

We must conclude then that conquest is destructive to the people whose form of government approaches to the free, or democratic; and that among the principles of their decline is that instinctive activity, pushing on to acquisitions dangerous to, and corruptive of the possessors.

On a review of the particular situation of Athens, from the casualties of the Persian war, and from the ill policy of the allies, it is not to be wondered at, that the leaders were influenced, or people mislead to a destructive system of insatiable conquest: opportunity courted them with an ever present, and assiduous smile; whilst

the,

the danger lurking in the obscure, was visible to none, or but to the strongest sight.

The annual subsidy entrusted to the administration of the Athenians amounted to four hundred and sixty talents, and from that and other resources ten thousand talents had gradually been amassed; Delos, indeed, was the place appointed for the deposit, but the treasurer was chosen, and resident at Athens, and his command of the monies was unaccounted for to the rest of the league. Not less firm was the sovereignty over the persons, than over the fortunes of the allies, whilst the military authority of Cimon was strengthened by the affection and gratitude of the Asiatic and other Greeks, whom he freed, whom he rescued, or whom he pardoned.

The city rebuilt on a new plan, and the fortifications erected on an improved principle, gave an ease and security to the inhabitants, wherein ingenuity found leisure for new arts of hostility or defence; whilst the Piræus was fraught with artificers, whom experience as seamen, had taught justly to estimate their work as shipbuilders, and to add to, or alter their mechanism from circumstantial recollection of deficiency or inconvenience.

Gold

Gold and silver abounded in the city: the captives were numerous, and the rich feared not to trust the menial arts, and their domestic concerns to the hands of slaves; whilst the citizens, whose fortunes were yet to make, gave up the hammer for the sword, or the plough for the par: easy was it to inspirit these greedy adventurers; and eager were the demagogues to use their influence,—embarked in the same pursuit of wealth, and urged by superior quest of glory.

Even the virtuous Aristides to conciliate the people to his designs, betrayed the constitution, and destroyed the well concerted balance of Solon, by favouring the Plebeian scale, whilst he annulled the exclusive pretensions of the ploutocracy to the archonship, and laid that dignity open to the commonalty.

Ambition is but a prouder species of avarice, —gain equally produces desire;—possession is equally wide of content; and the pursuit is equally indefinite;—for as the object is nor in the one, nor in the other case, enjoyed, it cannot satiate:—having received much, the Athenians soon learnt to demand more; and the crisis co-operating with their wishes, from an irregular and capricious exaction, they progressively adopted a fixed scheme of conquest, and a concerted

certed system of command. No longer insecure in their domestic concerns, many of the petty states grew tired of distant campaigns, and were desirous of repairing the ravages of past war by an assiduous attention to the arts of peace;—to such the Athenians permitted the wished-for retirement, provided that for the deficiency of men, they proportionally added to the pecuniary and naval subsidies: the ships they manned with their own citizens, and the monies they applied to the ornament of their city, or reserved it for future exigencies; and thus the nation became warlike, and the state wealthy. Others equally ill-satisfied with the continuance of hostilities, but more acute in penetrating the policy, and more bold in preventing the designs of the Athenians, harrangued in the haughty tone of opposition, and seceded from their command: but the prior attachment of many, and concessions of other cities had made the attempt nugatory, and at this crisis more fatal to the liberties of Greece, than even acquiescence; for each refractory state subdued under the pretext of delegated authority, became an accession to the particular forces of Athens, and was itself a means of more absolute exercise, and of a wider extent of power:—— thus the superiority at sea was strengthened by

the

the conquest of Ægina;—and thus the rebellion of the Thasians gave pretence for the seizure of their gold mines, and but served to encrease the funds of the already too powerful republic.

At the close of the Persian war many of the towns of Thrace, many of the Asiatic coast, most of the islands of the Ægean, the Cyclades, the very considerable tract of Eubæa, and various other districts in the vicinity and elsewhere, were tributary to the Athenians; nor did they rest contented with this dominion, but sought every occasion of dispute as a means of acquisition; and when discontent could not even coin a pretext for hostility, by holding forth a treacherous protection to each petty state, they found in its intestine commotions new means of usurpation, and in its foreign quarrels new subject of conquest. Whenever some ill-judging city thus called in their aid, gratitude at least demanded an acquiescence in the Athenian policy of sending their own supernumeraries, to inhabit part of the conquered or ceded territory; and too late such colony was found to be an ever-encroaching neighbour, and in times of trouble, an authoritative garrison. This mode of colonization was a favourite policy of the Athenian administration, and not restricted to countries, they were in treaty, ry, or at variance with; but by a cautious foresight, was extended to every remote spot, whereto the course of victory might direct their interests or designs: Pericles expedited a number of emigrants, who seized the country of the Sybarites, and under the appellation of Thurii, even in Italy, established a settlement mindful of the Athenian authority and name: these, if not effective of subordination in the adjacent parts by their power, might at least conciliate their alliance by attention and favor; and thus every way some force accrued to the original republic, from the measure:—for to attach powerful allies was another master-point in the Athenian councils;———with this view the pretensions of Inarus to the Ægyptian dynasty, were supported against the Persian;—and with this view, an attempt was made to reinstate Orestes in Thessaly.

The still keeping up the claim to the power of arbitrary taxation, under pretence that the Persian was meditating a renewal of hostilities; —the removal of the bank from Delos to Athens, —and the various other steps above-cited, tending to uncontrolable power, might well be supposed to rouse the attention of Sparta, and the other great republics of Greece:—the first important

portant state that coped with the Athenian arms was the Bæotian;—but in vain it would oppose their progress,—Myronides over-ran, and subdued the whole country to the very walls of Thebes. Corinth and other great cities were unable to enter into the conflict, whilst Athens, holding forth an insidious welcome to every factious tributary of any other state, divested it gradually of its strength, and contrasted fresh vigour with its decline. The Lacedæmonians would willingly have interposed, but the destruction of their city by an earthquake, and the desolation of their country, by the rebellious Helots, kept them too fully employed to give any effectual rebuff to the career of their rivals; —nay, they were even forced to ask their assistance to forward the siege of Ithomæ, where the insurgents had taken refuge; no sooner was the reinforcement arrived, but from suspicion it was remanded, and Athens disgusted at the insult, publicly disclaimed any further alliance with Lacedæmon: armies then came from Sparta with intent to succour the oppressed, and circumscribe the encroachments of this growing power; but of a force truly rather calculated to irritate, than to quell the enterprizing spirit of the Athenians: Bæotia indeed was recovered, but Samos

and

and many other places of importance, rested in the hands of the conquerors; and the Peloponesians rued dearly their interposition, Tolmides, and then Pericles, sailing with a mighty armament round the peninsula, and at various descents, burning the cities and desolating the country.

A general peace was at length negotiated, and took place, to the content of all:—for Athens too required leisure to methodize the wide extended rule she from good fortune, or good policy, had acquired.

CHAP.

THE man whom exercise hath trained to run easily with speed, will run with grace: the mind too not only becomes vigorous, but elegant, from the frequent use of its powers; what it hath begun, it will have the sagacity to finish; and what perfected, the spirit to refine: ——No longer satisfied with a trite road of practice, it will at length deviate into new paths, wherein to exercise its activity or strength; as it is allured by fairer prospects of pleasure, or expelled its old ways by obstacle or annoyance.

When a free state is in that point of its progression, that finished law and method have rendered interposition unnecessary, but to the agents of the commonwealth, the active mind disgusted with the sameness and facility of public practice, will recur to private life; and busily add convenience to necessaries, and luxury to convenience: each sense is then plied with enjoyment, till each object palls upon the taste; and successively the powers of art are called upon for new and more accomplished excellence to charm the ear, to fix the eye, or to enrapture the fancy.

Art has thus, in some countries, attained maturity, but its decline hath ever been rapid; for to rest contented with a stile of sculpture, or of literature, were to foregoe pursuit; and this being incompatible with mental inquietude, true science as well as every thing else, has had its vicissitudes, and yielded to that fondness for novelties which is the spring of all human undertaking; painting hath deviated into extravagancy or littleness; architecture hath lost its effect in finical ornament; poetry been buried in the quaintness of conceit; and even history in search of novel excellence hath wandered into the turgid, the marvellous, or the pretty.——When from the absolute perversion of government, politics are become dangerous, and a man no longer with safety can mingle in public administration, or securely, even agitate his private concerns; the intellect uneasy in sloth, will still recur to a proper object, and veiling the proscribed activity in Platonic speculation, or obviating its consequences with stoic firmness, will seek new life and motion from philosophy. Socrates, the first great moral preceptor, fell amidst the ruins of the Athenian republic,—and the sectaries of Zeno ho chiefly flourished under the tyranny of the Cæsars.

With an eye to the gradation of government, it is thus probable that art will forerun philosophy; and that the growing wealth, the pride of family, and love of distinction, may launch into the virtues of beneficence or vanities of patronage, previous to the dissipated luxury, productive finally of those revolutions, when the mind must, under the necessity of the times, seek some alleviation from silent system, or steel itself against actual evils by apathy, or blunt their force by anticipation:—says Tacitus,—*Postquam cædibus sævitum, et magnitudo famæ exitio erat, cæteri ad sapientiora convertere:* as the plenitude of power corrupts the despot, so the impotence of resistance forms the sage, nor under the casualty of their respective fortunes belongs it to ought; but to the divine eye, to penetrate the recess, and scan the merits of each character:—the tyrants may have been the better composition!—— O man of virtue, pity the criminal, and be humble!

Perhaps too, art may have the prior place from its more immediate connexion with the wants of mankind; the wooden bowl is polished to the hand, and delights the touch,——it is

engraved,

engraved, and pleases the eye:—the trunk in its elevation, naturally pushes forth new branches, and succeſſively ramifies on each ſhoot, till loſt in the minuteſt tendril!

Perhaps too philoſophy may come laſt in ſucceſſion, as being of that high and etherial caſt, as to require every previous experience and exerciſe to ſtrengthen and enlarge the mind, and render it at once capacious for its theories, and firm for its practice!

Perhaps too, when want is provided for,—every deſire ſerved,—even fancy ſatiated, and we can go no further;—to obviate diſapointment, we find out that we ought not—and pretend to adopt from choice, what we are driven to by neceſſity!

Free ſtates (it hath by many been obſerved) are the beſt nurſery-bed of the arts; and other ſtates (it will be obſerved) have ran a career ſomewhat ſimilar to that of Athens, and have known a period when emulation ſickening in the ſtagnation of public ſervices and duties, might be ſuppoſed to invigorate in other ſcenes of employment; and wherefore then (will it be asked) is the Athenian name ſo ſingularly preheminent in the annals of polite taſte and ingenious workmanſhip? The reader will remember, that ſoon

after

after the city was rebuilt, the people of Athens became principals in the Perſian war;—that the new intereſt was to be eſtabliſhed by ſome extraordinary exertion;—and that the gifts of fortune and of fame called forth every Athenian to the field, who had at heart his own honor and conſequence in the republic, or thoſe of the republic, in relation to Greece. From the dearth of young and active citizens, many of the menial trades fell to the numerous captives that thronged ſucceſſively from each victory: the warriours returning with all the pride of triumph, diſdained to practiſe the mechanical profeſſions, in common with their ſervants; to find them other employment, wherein none but freemen could be competitors, a decree paſſed, forbidding any ſlave the exerciſe of ſculpture or of painting;—and the liberal and the illiberal arts were thus for ever ſeparated at Athens: the moſt exalted ſpirit from that period, diſdained not the chiſel or the pallet; the labor as well as the deſign, equally ennobled genius; —the boldeſt theory thence was combined with the moſt delicate execution; nor was the time expended on the work any conſideration to the artiſt, whilſt renown was his object,—— or if avaricious, no price was eſteemed too high for a

noble

noble and finished performance;—if I mistake not, Pliny tells us, that the Laocoon took up the lives of a father and his two sons;—a work from which the most elaborate Dutchman might learn to finish, the most correct draftsman might study precision, and the most sublime poet invention and idea!

Another circumstance which conduced particularly to the refinement and progress of the arts at Athens, was the timely administration of one who from nature and education had every requisite of judicious taste, and possessed at once the most unbounded power, and most liberal spirit that ever ennobled patronage. Pericles the son of the Xantippus renowned for the defeat of the Persians at Mycale, comes not at present to our view in the character of minister, but of patron;—his mind opened by the subtilties of his preceptor Anaxagoras, and polished by his intercourse with the accomplished Aspasia; exercised by the ingenious sophistry of the sage, and refined by the erudite delicacy and elegance of his no less philosophical mistress,—it grew flexible and capacious,—it became benevolent and luxurious,—luxurious in those objects which through the sense awaken the fancy, and enrapture the soul with the contemplation of symme-
trie

tric beauty:——to feel this divine, this harmonic sentiment the mind must be in unison with, and beautiful (if I may so express it) as, its object;—it must have all the pliable variety, all the enthusiastic wanderings a visionary tutor could exercise it to; and all the yielding temper, the refined judgment, the squeamish nicety of taste, (in a word) the melody of finished character which may result, and can result only, from the converse of a lovely, and beloved woman!

With a taste for the liberal sciences and arts, Pericles (how illicitly I will not at present urge) enjoyed the most ample means of recompensing desert, and of fostering genius: the bank of the general contributions had been removed from Delos, and no immediate exigency demanding the application of these monies to the common cause, he converted them to the purposes of embellishing the city, and with an assiduity that soon rendered Athens the ornament, as it had been the bulwark of Greece: Nor did Pericles find it difficult to gain the assent of his countrymen, to this misuse of the public funds; Athens was a mistress endeared by loss, and whose value was enhanced by the difficulties of redemption, and no citizen grudged to dissipate

sipate his own, or even to trespass on his neighbour's patrimony,—to deck out her beauties, and give new lustre to her name.

The immortal statuary Phidias was made superintendant of the public works, and by his fame drew together the first artists of Greece, and without envy, gave due encouragement to all,—" for envy (as Pericles nobly observes in his funeral oration)——comes not but from somewhat inferior to its object."

Public edifices of the richest and grandest structure were every where raised;—what the magnificence of these buildings was, may be surmised from the sum of a thousand talents, or an hundred and eighty thousand pounds sterling expended solely on the temple of Minerva, and that at a time when, from the multitude of slaves, labor was almost gratuitous: in this temple, called the Parthenion, stood a statue of the goddess, thirty cubits high, wrought in ivory by the hand of Phidias, and profusely decorated with gold;—the precious metal used for the figure of a victory, affixed to the breastplate, amounted in weight alone, to forty talents:—I have dwelt on the richness of material particularly, for surely the workmanship of these times need not be insisted on, when (if I

may

may fo exprefs it) we have the many living examples thereof in the Florentine gallery, and in the Belvidere court at Rome.

Polygnotus too and others at this period excelled much in painting: a mere enumeration of their works, not agreeing with the tenor of this effay, muft give way to a digreffion on a lefs trite, though much queftioned fubject,— Was the art of the ftatuary antecedent to the painters? I am convinced that it was, and with the learning of the German Winckelman on my fide, will on this point difpute with even the ingenious Mr. Webb.—To talk of the perfect knowledge of drawing, as previoufly neceffary to the formation of a figure which on every bearing and in every light, was to have the juft outline of nature, implies a very partial comprehenfion of the poffible beginnings of the art;— rather fhould I fuppofe (and the relicts of the higheft antiquity aid my fuppofition) that the firft models of the human figure depended for their correctnefs on the momentary idea, and precife vifion of the artift, and that he plaiftered on his clay, or pared its prominencies, till his eye was fatisfied with the fimilitude. There were indeed fuch ftatues as the Ægyptian, hewn

out

out on diagram rather than defign, with acute angles, no grace of limb, no motion, no compofition, but an exact and fcrupulous length of bone and conformity of proportions: Dædalus the Athenian, on thefe granite mummies, I can well imagine to have firft worked, and to have improved them without the ftudy of drawing, or the affiftance of ought other original than nature;——to have feparated the limbs from their rigid unity with the trunk,——to have enlarged fome, and to have diminifhed other parts, till the nice gradations of mufcle, and their modulation to attitude, were founded on uniform experience and more exact obfervation.

The portraits of Semiramis and her hufband on the walls of Babylon will be quoted from Diodorus, and the lovers fhadow penciled round by his miftrefs, will be cited from Pliny, and many other tales, and much reafoning may be brought to prove the antiquity of painting; and if I will not allow art to originate from that quarter, the conceffion will be expected of me at leaft, that fculpture and painting may be nearly coeval; but not even this can I agree to; —nor was the palace of Alcinous, nor other
kingly

kingly hall decked by the lavish song of Homer, therein decorated with pictures, but——.

> Two rows of stately dogs on either hand,
> In sculptur'd gold and labor'd silver stand:
> These Vulcan form'd with art divine, to wait
> Immortal guardians of Alcinous gate;
> Alive each animated frame appears.   POPE.

—Nor was the temple or house of Solomon adorned with pictures.--In all the Eastern metaphors of the earlier holy writ, I remember not one exemplification from painting:—but says the divine canon,—" Thou shalt not make to thyself any " graven image:"—from the figure of man to form a similar figure, was surely more obvious, than to deceive the sense by that complicated art which gives a just swell and relative depressure to a plane surface.—The statue had a simple and obvious original.—The man who first stripped the bark from the tree, and smoothed the knotty trunk, was in his way to that art, which afterwards stretched to the formation of an Apollo.

At the time when sculpture was at the highest pitch, then painting began to emulate its excellence; much it was to seek without the pale of imitation, but much too it was to borrow from the prior art; colour and its contingencies of light

light and shade, it was to seek for in nature, but the precise outline it could more readily copy from the correct and unvarying models of a Phidias or Alcamenes; from attention to such finished performances design soon attained a degree of perfection, which no modern work can be supposed to give a just idea of;—when Pliny tells me that—*Ambire debet se extremitas, et sic definere ut promittat alia post se, ostendatque quæ occultat*;—I confess my eye is but ill-satisfied with even the Sestine chapel. Whilst we allow the superiority of design to the ancient painters, let us not extravagantly deal them out every accomplishment of the profession: from the old poets, and from the antiquarians, Ælian, Pausanias, and others, I think one may gather that the ancient artists delighted much in single figures, and that their single figures had all the animation that colour and design could produce; but their more crowded pictures seem to have been of a frigid, or of an extravagant composition: they knew not the technical propriety and disposition of planes; nor do they appear to have been well acquainted with the beauties of effect modulated on the varieties of the aerial medium;—in the picture of the battle of Marathon, besides a very particular delineation of all that passed in that memorable

morable field, the Persian fleet too was descried from afar, *and Cinægirus retaining the vessel with his teeth.* Their characters must generally, I think, have been better in the detail, than in the groupe, and the figures, rather than the picture, have been the object of admiration. Though a passage is cited from Vitruvius, mentioning a scene as old as the times of Æschylus, drawn *apparently* on just principles of optics, and on which Anaxagoras wrote a treatise;—and though Eupompus (we are expressly told) was of opinion, that a knowledge of geometry was necessary to an exact delineation of the objects in nature, yet cannot I coincide in the idea that the ancients were masters of a regular and systematic perspective :—particular instances belong rather to the side of exception, than of rule;—when we are told of one particular scene, I should imagine it to be singularity which recommended it to notice;—when we are told that one Eupompus was of such, or such an opinion, it implies, I think, that the generality were not.

Nicetas, as we learn from Cicero's academics, and others, as we learn from the first book of Lucretius, had a just idea of the figure of the earth; but such system not being the adoption of the age, it is not to be placed to the account of its erudition.

erudition.—It thus little furthered the progress of natural philosophy; and as little might the opinion of one individual artist, prove the advancement of art.

Without mathematical knowledge much may be done,—a building may be tolerably drawn,— a flying line well conducted from mere observation,—and without any fixed point of sight or diagram from rule and compass, an acute and steady eye may learn to well distinguish the position, situation, and distance of objects, by showing their proper planes in their proper forms, and marking the regular and just diminution;—but the perspective part of design is then dependant for its accuracy rather on the artist, than on the art,—and is liable to gain or lose, as his delicacy of vision corrects, or his dullness or inattention perverts it; whilst, if founded on known and invariable principles, a mechanic—a very bricklayer can scarcely err: that the ancients had no such just theory, is sufficiently apparent, I think from the pictures discovered in the theatre of Herculaneum, and town of Pompeii; nor will it avail to say that they were done when painting was in its decline; —the more noble branches of the science, it may not be just therefore to question from the examples

amples before us, but the more mechanical parts of the profession might be supposed to have gained ground, as the sublimer fell into decay;—had perspective ever been reduced to just principles, it would have been perfected on the ruins of the art it was founded on,——its difficulties would have been explored, novel singularities have exercised its truths, and the beauties of design would have been succeeded by professional subtilty and trick:—nor will it avail to assert, that these works were of some inferior, some provincial hand.—The frequent residence of the emperors and Roman nobility on this coast might authorize contradiction,—but it is unnecessary, as it proves nothing, whilst even in this country (a country by no means famous in the chapter of art) not even a sign-post can be produced whereon are depicted the upper and under surface of the same solid, a circumstance not uncommon in the otherwise neatly and finely executed relicts of ancient painting.

CHAP.

CHAP. III.

THE manners of men in private life are subject to the censure or approbation of every one; for every one arrived at maturity thinks he hath seen enough of private life, and is apt to deduce a general theory from his private practice, to which whatever doth not conform, is set at naught; with him complacency hath but one sort of good-breeding, and good morals but one sort of decency; what is good, and what is proper is definable by his own habits of conversation, and his indignation is raised at the very supposition, that there may be other manners as well as his own effective of grace, chearfulness, and improvement to society:——To such the author might appear sophistical, or, at best, visionary, who should assert,—" That the American wood
" and French court are regions equally barba-
" rous;—who should pretend,—that men are
" the best situated, when in that golden mean
" of civilization, which inculcates the genuine
" social duties of hospitality, unadulterated by
" new-

" new-fangled ceremonies; and influences to mu-
" tual affiftance and fervices, untainted by falfe and
" barbarous diftinctions and interefts;—who fhould
" argue, that at fuch period affociates were not
" only more friendly, but more companionable;—
" that the virtues not fhining doubtfully under the
" infincerity of compliment, were open for all to
" chufe, and to attach themfelves to, thofe the
" moft congenial with their own;—that converfa-
" tion had more varieties from thofe of character,
" not being polifhed off;—and more fcience from
" the youthful years not being facrificed to ufelefs
" or trivial accomplifhments, or to the vicious
" practice of exterior benevolence with mental re-
" fervation;—who fhould fay, that, in what is now
" called fuperior or refined company, rarely ought
" but trivial queftions are debated with candour
" and with learning:—Ignorance begets incohe-
" rency, and incoherency warmth; —politics,—
" nay, even philofophy grows paffionate!—not
" having explored the great truths, and fixed their
" principles of good and bad, of right and wrong.
" —Thefe modern men (to ufe a metaphor of the
" fublime, the virtuous Shaftfbury) when launched
" in the current of reafoning, ignorant of its depths
" and courfe, alarmed, catch with hafte at the firft

M " twig,

"twig, and with all their strength struggle to af-
"sist its weakness, little weening that the same
"force would land them safely on the shore;—
"some point in argumentation is thus casually and
"unmeaningly caught at, and with obstinacy,
"defended against some one, whilst both, if exer-
"cised and friendly, swimmers might down the
"current have floated on to the terra firma of
"truth:"—the queer sentiments of such old cynic
(if such there be) I submit willingly to the polite
abuse of the reader; but in return I expect a
concession on his side, and that for once, at
least, he will forget his own rules of refinement,
and prepare to admit, that with a demeanor different from his own, an Athenian may have had
the requisites for rendering his society mirthful,
easy, and instructive.

The frequent assemblage of the people on the
public concerns must have made every one con-
versant in political subjects; and the minds too
of men must thence have become strong, and
fitted for abstruse discourse, penetrating in dis-
quisitions of serious moment, lively in common
chat, and communicative at all times; for no
restriction silenced the boldest champion of
discontent, or merriest advocate of scandal.

The

The dominion of the seas and general spirit of commerce allured several to foreign parts. Travel thus broke in upon national prejudice; and the residence of the many strangers at this general mart on business, or for pleasure, or for both, opened the minds of all, and brought together; as it were, the notions of the known world to enrich the mental stock of the Athenians. They thus educated, comprized others, as well as Greeks, within the circle of their benevolence: their very slaves were treated with a partiality proportionate to their merit; they were cloathed without distinction, like citizens;—to strike or even insult another's slave was highly penal; and some of natural elegance of manners, or peculiar erudition, were even admitted to a familiar participation of the table. If one may extract any just opinion from cotemporary and other authors, I should say,—that the merry and wise never kissed each other with more tempered cordiality, than at this period, in Athens: in a country where a mindful drinker * was proverbial for a dangerous man, good fel-

lowship

* —μισεω μναμνα συμποτων. V. Plutarchi Symp. 2.

lowship could have been no rarity; nor where a harlot dogmatized, could philosophy have been out of vogue.

The fine gentleman will object their grossness of conversation, which he will observe is obvious from many ancient writers, and more particularly the open indecencies of their great comic poet, who assuredly wrote conformably to the taste of his auditors;—to such it might be said, (and the severe and virtuous stoic † would say) that propriety of language is merely a matter of convention: and that words are not libertine, if the sentiment is not so; nor a vicious sentiment proper, however cautious the language it is couched in.

The gallant will object—that the Athenian ladies were much confined, and prohibited the festivity of a promiscuous society;—— but the courtezans were admitted, and without discredit admitted; and where there were such as Aspasia,

(with

---

† —Placet stoicis suo quamque rem nomine apellare, sic enim disserunt, " nihil esse obscenum nihil turpe dictu; nam si quod in obscenitate flagitium, id aut in re esse, aut in verbo; nihil esse tertium; in re non est, &c. multo minus in verbis, si enim quod verbo significatur turpe non est, verbum quod significat turpe esse non potest." T. Ciceron. Ep. fam. l. 9. ep. 22.

(with reverence be it spoken) the abfence of the matrons might not have been fo deplorable.

The epicure will object—the proverb of an Athenian feaft—ever bearing application to fomething very wide of profufion—will point out Pericles going forth to a friend's dinner, with his portion of eatables born after him by a flave, and then laughingly perhaps will remind you of a college tutor on his march to fupper, ftrutting before the decrepit bearer of his pipe and commons :——this is raillery and not argument ;— a greater glutton in good converfation, than in good eating, I feel not the force of it, nor think it worth the anfwering.

Domeftic parcimony is far from incompatible with public magnificence : the citizens of Athens had yet fomewhat of the patriot,—were yet capable of fympathifing with the glory of the commonwealth, and of facrificing thereto fome portion of more private interefts, and more felfifh defires : their forefathers loved their country,—they were proud of it,—and pride for a time proped up the ruins of that fabric which virtue had raifed. The firft fuitors of the fair miftrefs Athens were fentimentally attached to the foul; —(as in the motto prefixed to this treatife, Ifocrates

crates emphatically calls the spiritual tenor of the institution)——Their successors too were yet constant to the fair; but it was a grosser passion for the sensible object, and was no longer displayed by a brave and knight-like assiduity of service, and a subserviency of morals to the pure and correct pattern of the republic, but was shown in a prodigality of ornament and a profusion of wealth corruptive of, and ruinous to the very patriot-love that lavished it; for an attachment to sensible objects passes almost with the novelty, and the mind thereby degenerates into a vicious levity.

When the Athenians began to view with rapture and pride the beauties of their city, the splendid array of their fleets, and to glory in their grandeur and opulence,—they gloried indeed in what was external and quickly perishable, for what was internal and lasting, but still something in common was at heart;—nay, the cement of the public weal for a moment seemed more binding and strong;—as if lock'd up by a frost, but to perish with the dissolution of the season: in a former period, men gave up their very sustenance, their very lives for the well-being, for the life of the republic; they now made the smaller sacrifice of private to public luxury;

luxury, and lived thriftily at home, to add to the pomp of the festival, to the apparel of the theatre, or to the decoration of the city: self-love indeed, by a penetrating eye, might be discovered in its passage homeward, it seemed to have withdrawn from the extreme circle of the social system, and might be supposed shortly to plot for itself, and confuse and break the compact with jarring interests and designs.

Xenophon in his treatises on the revenues and on the state of Athens, gives us a very unfavorable account of the aggregate manners of the commonalty, but it was of a some-what after period of which he wrote, and moreover, he is to be listened to with caution, for he was a professed enemy of the republic, and often asserts from prejudice, what even at this distance of time may be readily confuted:——he tells us that the people bore not with reproof, nor ever admitted any sharp touches relative to their conduct; but this is contradicted both by the famous satirical picture of * Parrhasius, and almost every

---

* Voluit namque varium, iracundum, injurium, inconstantem; eundem exorabilem, clementem, misericordem, excelsum, gloriosum, humilem, fugacemque et omnia pariter ostendere.   Pliny, L. 35.

every play, and more particularly the knights of Ariſtophanes, (a paſſage in which, by the by, proves the knowledge of letters very general, for the man who keeps the pudding-ſtall, confeſſes he hath had no good education, *for he could only read and write*).—Xenophon hath ever ſeemed to me but a doubtful name;—for, tho' eminent as a ſoldier, he was in mercenary ſervice; though ſkilled as a ſtateſman, yet an atpoſtate from his country; though great as a philoſopher, yet meanly envious of the greater Plato.

Whoever would develope a national character, let him contemplate it in the laws and regulations of the ſtate, the nature of its dominion abroad, and the tenor of its conſtitution at home; let him reflect on their combination with the arts, with the religion,——nay, with the very face, and climate of the country; with theſe let him compare hiſtorical facts, and if he hath candidly and acutely purſued the ſpeculation, he will have a ſet of manners before him very near the truth, and which ſhould cautiouſly cede to even a cotemporary opinion, and however reſpectable.

CHAP.

CHAP. IV.

AN interval of peace hath given us leisure to digress a while, and we have beguiled the idle hour in researches after domestic and general refinements. We left the Athenians studying the arrangement and command of the vast force they had acquired; we are soon to view it on the march, but previously let us array this armament, and mark the particularities whence may be presumed its discomfiture or success, let us examine the character of the leader, and the numbers and ordonnance of the whole.

Pericles was ennobled by descent from the Xantippus who commanded the fleet at Mycale, this and his own personal accomplishments, and more particularly his affability, and a natural readiness of speech, which by study he had improved into a most refined eloquence, made him an early favourite of the people; but by the wiser remarked as a transcendant character, which might sometime bear the commonwealth from its proper biass, and the admirable qua-

lities

lities of which were to be regarded as the more dangerous, in proportion to the public favor and notice they attracted; his person too was said to resemble that of Pisistratus, and light as this circumstance should seem, it was the weight that set the people's minds agoing in search of other similarities which never were, or never would have been remarked, but for the first ground-work on which fancy wrought, of a semblance of voice and physiognomy: Pericles finding himself thus the object of suspicion, and his manners, and even gait, a text on which each cautious republican was to rouse the attention and free spirit of the people, he determined to elude the effects of the public apprehension, by withdrawing for a time from those assemblies wherein he was regarded with so fearful and wary an eye: He left the city for the camp, and strived to substitute the name of a hardy soldier, for that of an artful and plotting citizen; to simulate and dissimulate were now become his necessary study, and so deeply did he profit of the theory, that on his return, he managed to ingratiate himself and secure a party, before his opponents were even aware that from their remissness or mistake, he had taken a

strong

strong hold in the affections of the people, and which their united powers or policy were insufficient to force or to entice him from: In vain the lavish spirit of Cimon, with feasts and shows, attempted to rival him in the good favor of the commonalty; Pericles opposed prodigality to prodigality, and the sole result of the contest was further licentiousness in the state:—in vain the honest sense and valour of Thucydides were patronised by the nobles, and set up to cope with the pretensions of this rising genius———— " when I throw him (said Thucydides) he says he is not down, and they believe him, even when on the ground:" with his eloquence he carried all before him, and imbittered by the repeated attacks of the higher class, he turned its whole current to sap the bulwark of the aristocracy; licentiousness then poured in with eddies and whirlpools, with streams and with counter-streams, wherein indeed himself was found (but alone found) an adequate pilot to the commonwealth,—from whom none could take the helm, and with whom the vessel was wholly to perish.

—When manners were incorrupt: when justice ruled at home, and equity abroad; when in the purity of the institution, all were considered

by

by each, and each by none; when the individual ſtate leaned to philanthrophy, as the individual to the ſtate; and moral fitneſs was extended to national intereſts, and the rule of national conduct, adminiſtration required no refinement;—even as men deviated from (if ever they were bleſt by) ſuch virtuous ſyſtem, ſtill a ſound intellect and a firm ſpirit were for a while equal to the miniſtry of public affairs: but now to harmonize all the jarring and diſcordant elements which ſociety was broken into,—to keep together and direct together this heterogeneous and uncemented maſs, without change, and without loſs, required an art unknown to former times,—an art reſerved for the genius of Pericles:—to corrupt, and to rule by corruption;—to extract unanimity from diſcordant paſſions;—to prop ſuccumbing valour with pride;—to deduce the patriot virtues from the animoſities of party;—to build a ſyſtem of dependence on vanity, and for ſubordination to ſubſtitute dependance; to draw plenty from diſſipation, and make the comforts and competence of the many, proceed from the extravagance of the few;—in foreign marts to balance commodity by manufacture, and the utilty of manufacture by novelty or elegance;—to purchaſe armies with wealth, and recover wealth

with

with armies, or make negotiation fupply the deficiencies of both;—thefe were the arts of this great man, great may be faid, for the greateft in thefe refpects have thought him a fit object of their emulation,—well were it if they confidered too the other qualities and merits which raifed this character to the high preheminence it holds! —Pericles was truly what Cato faid of Pompey.

———————————————— falvâ
Libertate, potens; et folus, plebe paratâ,
Privatus, parere fibi.

—He encroached not on the liberties of the republic, nor though he diffipated the funds of the ftate, did he raife a fortune on its bankruptcy; as he ufed it to conciliate, fo at times did he employ his eloquence to reprove and chaften the turbulency of the populace; as from ambition he banifhed, fo from virtue he recalled his competitor Cimon;—as rivalfhip loft ground, he honored his rivals; and finally fought to reftore the patrician influence, and anew balance the commonwealth: to gain the lead in public affairs, he had much perplexed, but no one knew better how to unravel them; he had ever fome resource for the distresses, some safeguard in the dangers, some honorable means of colouring over the discredit of the republic.

Arts and science flourished under his patronage, public spirit was countenanced, and the general welfare and safety (as far as was compatible with the general corruption) were attended to with a happy insight and resolute practice: as the force of Athens sickened from the depravity of her citizens, he medicated the weakness, and substituting art for strength, taught her to act with a skill and vigilance more than equal to manly prowess:—the warriour who trembled under the shield, might securely throw his javelin from the rampart, unsteady in the field, he might yet be dexterous on the seas; the subordinate states being mostly or islanders or maritime, thereby were more easily to be kept under, and an enemy under the like predicament more easily annoyed; and if desolation was spread through the territory of Attica, its fleets with sudden and unprepared for invasion might make a descent on the enemy's coasts, and the balance of conquest and depredation for a time be equally held;——for a time I say,—for arts may be acquired

quired by those who have them not, but virtue rarely be recovered by those who have lost it.

It is said that Pericles, or to screen some past malversation, or to make his abilities necessary for the future, engaged his country in a war;—that to trust to fortifications and fleets was the system of war he adopted, is certain;—that he was the immediate or the sole cause of the rupture between Athens and Sparta, is much, and with much reason to be doubted: Thucydides expressly tells us, " that the dominion of Athens was become too absolute and extensive to be any longer regarded with passive envy by the great rival states; they thought even their own liberties endangered, and if they found not, were ready to coin some pretext for hostilities, and league together to pluck the eagle's wing ere she gained a pitch above the flight of vengeance. The ostensible history is as follows.

Epidamnus owed its settlement to united colonies from Corinth and from Corcyra; dissention had thus an original germe in this little state, which finally burst forth, and in the commotion, many of the most noted and most wealthy of the citizens were compelled to fly the fury of the populace and take shelter in the neighbouring but

bar-

barbarous district of the Taulantii: these people they persuaded to aid their design of forcibly reinstating themselves in their country; when the townsmen inveterately bent against their return, sent to Corcyra for succour wherewith to repel the attack, and drive the assailants back to the woods; Corcyra refusing assistance, they then applied to Corinth as being the joint parent state, where their plea was admitted, and forthwith a subsidy voted to back their pretensions and party: Corcyra alarmed at this interposition of Corinth, and fearful lest the colony of Epidamnus should now totally recur from its protection to that of its rival, thought fit to take a part in its affairs, and dispatch a fleet in support of the exiles; this and the Corinthian armaments met, and the latter being worsted, the flame had caught, which afterwards burst in conflagration over Greece: Epidamnus was now lost sight of, Corinth sought to revenge itself on Corcyra, and Corcyra deeming itself alone unequal to the conflict, applied to the alliance of Athens: the Corinthian emissaries met them fraught with arguments evincive of the justice of their cause; but the Corcyreans made a better plea to the ambition of their auditors;—They were islanders,—

their

their navy was powerful,—they were situated conveniently for the invasion of the nether side of the Peloponnese,—or of Italy,—or of Sicily,—or thence of the whole borders of the Mediterranean: such an opportunity might not again occur, and was not now therefore to be past over; some respect however had the Athenians for appearances, and not to seem in the eye of Greece the first abettors of fresh hostility they concluded a merely defensive treaty with the Corcyreans; but to make a defensive treaty with a people already in arms, was surely equivalent to a declaration of war. The Corinthians unable to cope alone with these united powers addressed the Spartans, and roused them from their lethargy with a tale of this new accession to their rivals, the dangerous avidity of further possession thence discoverable in the Athenians, and their own loss of that power and estimation in Greece, which was so gloriously bequeathed them by their forefathers at Plataea.

Sparta now sent to Athens, and Athens sent back to Sparta, and successive negotiation was agitated, but in such a manner as proved either to be in search only of some colouring for their animosity, and some means of involving others

others too in the dispute, and making the rupture general.

. Pericles at length plainly told his countrymen,—" that to cede the minutest point in debate, was to give up national honor without providing for national security; that their pusillanimity apparent on a trivial concession would merely draw on further and more important requisitions;—and that as well as more becoming, it was more advantageous to reject in the first instance, and show a spirit, that at least would ensure the confidence of their allies, and submission of their tributaries :—He displayed to them their wealth :—ten thousand talents were then in the treasury;——six hundred they received annually in tribute; the temples were rich in ornaments of gold; and the massive spoils of the Persian camp were ready in exigency to be melted down :——he made known to them their force;—their army was numerous and well appointed; and their navy, amounting to three hundred sail, was all equipped, and ready for embarkation :——he showed them the extent and advantage of their dominion;——from Corcyra and Zacynthus on the one side, and Eubœa on the other, they seemed to embrace the whole

whole Grecian seas; they possessed the vast cluster of the Cyclades; and to these, and to other islands of the Ægean had lately added the capital acquisition of Samos;——on the continent their possessions seemed so happily scattered, that they well might be imagined chosen garrisons of Greece: they had at command Acarnania on the confines of the Ætolian, and Platæa on the borders of the Bæotian territory, and Messenia in the extreme of the Peloponnese; and Amphipolis and Eion and other cities in Thrace; and they had the Chersonese and Hellespont; and they had parts of Caria and Ionia, on the Asiatic coast; Doria in the northern extremity of Greece was theirs; and themselves were situated in the very center of the field of war, ready to dispatch succour or annoyance to each point of the circle: with these resources, and with this empire Athens could not brook concession;—a defiance ensued;—and war was prepared for on all sides. —Hostilities commenced with an attempt to surprise Platæa; the town was taken and was recovered; many of the agressors were slain, and many remained captive within the walls; the Theban army then desolating the district around, approached the city to support the enterprize of their countrymen; whose failure and captivity being made acquainted with, they entered into treaty for their lives, and promised to desist from further devastation, on condition that their citizens were remanded on the army's retreat from the country; these terms were agreed to, and the Thebans withdrew; but no sooner were they withdrawn, than the Platæans put to death their prisoners; and this act of atrocious and wanton perfidy, portentive of all its horrors and cruelty, opened the Peloponnesian war.

Both Athens and Sparta sent to sollicit the alliance of the Persian king, who warily for the present, listened to their several pretensions; it was his interest to let the contending states waste the very marrow of their strength, ere he accorded any succour, and then by supporting the one or the other, as their weakness called for his aid to raise them again for the fight, he finally might with facility oppress together both the combatants.

The subordinate states of Athens were strictly under its command; they paid their tribute and service; they had no dissentient voice; and their fleets and armies were headed by Athenians;—thus they were submissive, but they were faithless.

The

The Spartans were at the head of an alliance embarked in one common cause, but with various and independant interests; thus, though steady to the general purpose, yet often on particulars they were diffentient.

The Spartans in the several cities under their sovereignty placed an oligarchy, and the form of government seemed to secure a quiet and easy administration, but the people were not in their interests, and in a crisis of danger co-operated not with ardour and spirit.

The Athenians fostered their own democracy in each little district of their dominion, but with so many restrictions and reservations in favor of their own supremacy, that whilst the Aristocratics were disgusted at the licentiousness, the popular advocates were equally irritated by the controul of government, and only the ubiquity of the fleet, and often not even that, could insure the faithful adherence of their tributaries. The distinctions of opulence and family, and the strength of numbers occasioned at times the most bloody commotions in every town of Greece, and as the demagogues, or the patrician influence got the better; the parties respectively

opened

opened their gates to the Athenian, or to the confederate forces.

The Peloponnesians were numerous and warlike but not wealthy, and thus were bold and powerful in sudden invasion, but not being provided for a long campaign, their force quickly wasted, and the excursion though impetuous,—not being sustained, was indecisive.

Pericles was aware of the force and of the weakness of the enemy, and not attempting to oppose the frequent inroads into Attica, left the country open to devastation, and sought to repair the loss by reprisals made by his fleets. The peninsula could double the musters of Athens, but Athens had resources that equalled the lesser to the greater number: she excelled in arts offensive, and defensive; her great wealth supplied necessaries, and her expeditions were marked by vigour and perseverance; her fleets wafted her troops where they were not expected, and of course were not to be resisted;—nor prowess, nor thousands could balance these advantages:—it was not till after receiving subsidies from the Persian treasury, and a lesson of naval affairs dearly purchased by repeated and bloody defeat, that Sparta gained the final superiority in this long contention.

Animosity

Animosity was in these times carried to the most horrid excess; party in each little state abetted the carnage of the great civil broil; when any town capitulated, private enmity and political dissention demanded the murder of those whom national hostility had spared;—— well were it, if only some of the more zealous republicans, or more esteemed and distinguished nobles were the victims;—often a whole people were massacred,—the Platæans, the Melians and many others were after conquest deliberately put to the sword,——nay!—*a long and much debated edict passed at Athens* ——"to extirpate without respect to sex or age, every citizen of the noble and populous Mitylene!"—men's minds (says Thucydides) at length became totally depraved and habituated or to fraud, from the necessities, or to cruelty, from the examples of the times; treachery was foresight, temerity was valour, every vice put on the name of some virtue, and every virtue was degraded by some apellation, that brought danger or contempt on its adherents; when any party got the better, the first slaughter was so horrid, that on a reverse of fortune, the second should seem but justice, was not the second encreased to that

pitch

pitch of cruelty, as to make the first comparatively innocent!

The herdsmen flying their defenceless villages, thronged to the fortified towns, and there served to mingle in the tumult and feed the appetite of carnage: to be idle is to be vicious, and habits of vice and idleness are not readily foregone, and thus was honest industry in a great measure lost, and Greece no longer to be the rich and labored country, which of yore nurtured so many beauteous commonwealths: these multitudes of men crouding all together within walls, their temperament of body as well as of mind was vitiated, and desperation found new subject for its horrors and extravagance in pestilence and famine:——who hath not read of the memorable plague at Athens?——Then Pericles too died; perhaps it hath been well for the republic, had he never been born!—but his death was equally fatal to it as his life: none other knew how to medicate the ills he had occasioned; he had used the people to the voice of a demagogue;—his indeed, as it ever urged some just and useful plan, so was it a charm, that like Aaron's rod, swallowed up all others, and with a superior magic kept the assemblies consistently to his purpose: on his death a thousand

sand pretenders arose, and with rival arts and equal weakness perplexed the public councils, disunited the people, and led them to ruin and destruction.

On the barren rock of Sphacterium, four hundred and twenty of the first warriours of Sparta were surrounded by the Athenian fleet; many of them were killed, and the remainder after a sharp contest surrendered at discretion: Sparta humiliated by the loss sued to Athens for peace; Athens for a while haughtily rejected the proposal, but Brasidas with the specious proclamation of general liberty, having gained many of the towns of Thrace, and Thessaly, and with successful arms, or more successful clemency dailily bringing over others from the Athenian dominion or alliance, they at length ceded to the request, and agreed to a truce of one year, wherein they might have leisure to concert a treaty, the ground-work of which was to be, the exchange of the prisoners from Sphacterium for the cities which Brasidas had got possession of, whether by conquest, or from defection. This truce was quickly infringed, Brasidas still pursuing his victories in pretended ignorance of the cessation of arms: The Athenians at length sent an army to oppose his progress under the command

mand of one Cleon, a braggart, who had talked himself into office by depreciating real merit, and lauding his own and that of the people: the cowardice and ignorance of this Cleon brought deftruction on the army committed to his care, though fuperior in appointment and numbers to the enemy: the Athenian forces were cut to pieces, but on the other fide, the death of Brafidas feemed almoft a balance to the victory; for though others might be found to lead the army, not one could pretend to that perfonal intereft he had acquired throughout the country, by a perfeverance in the virtues (fo uncommon to thofe times) of candour, ftrict faith, mercy, and beneficence.

Both parties now again recurred to negociation, and a peace was finally concluded between Athens and Sparta: thefe fovereign ftates too haftily put their fignatures to a treaty, fufficiently explicit indeed with refpect to themfelves, but too little provident of their acceffaries in the war, whofe welfare and even fafety were no part of the conditions.

Moft of the fubordinate ftates during the courfe of hoftilities, had at fometime wavered in their faith,——fome had been marked by the moft
bloody

bloody perfidy,—sedition had raged in all, and the rancour of party suppressed, but not subdued, was ready to take the lead anew, as invited by the opportunities of power:—how should the confederate cities thus stained with the crimes of treachery and cruelty, return without stipulated terms of oblivion and forgiveness to their former, and now offended masters? Democracies had become oligarchies, and aristocratic governments popular;—were these states to be lightly bartered, for the Athenian to depress the nobles of the one, and the Spartans to raise those of the other, whilst private revenge of the aggrieved but now powerful party, on either side finished the work of depopulation, which war had so successfully begun? The dissentient cities implored, and met with disregard; they remonstrated, and met with evasions; they threatened,—and Athens and Sparta determined against further dispute between themselves entered into an offensive and defensive alliance, the very name of which they deemed sufficient to silence every murmur of the malecontents, and necessitate them to a discretionary submission: Argos and Corinth however taking the lead, formed a confederacy where-

wherewith to oppose the united powers and force them to some concession in their favor.

A second war was now likely to break out, more bloody than the first. Athens was become Spartan, and Sparta Athenian, the subordinates of either had broken their engagements, and embarked in a new cause; all had changed sides;—hostilities now leaned still nearer to civil discord;—the deluge again threatened the fields, but from a still more envenomed source; —well doth the poet say—

———" Alta sedent civilis vulnera dextræ!

Perhaps happily for the generality of Greece, though fatally for our republic, the ambition of an individual broke in upon these new compacts and roused the old hereditary flame between Lacedæmon and Athens.—" this, said Alcibiades, this is the time to humble your old, your haughty rivals;—go head the Argive league, and soon you will be at the head of Greece." His eloquence abetted by falsehoods, and every art and intrigue the orator's policy could suggest, at length prevailed with the assembly; and the alliance with Argos was concluded on: Argos

not

not long afterwards ceded to Sparta, but soon again its oligarchy being overthrown, it returned to its engagements and the establishment of a popular government cemented its union with Athens, who to other advantages accruing from this mighty accession of strength, might at length be said to have a footing in the Peloponnese.

CHAP.

CHAP. V.

OF the various adventurers who migrated into Attica, many (as we observed) had sailed from distant coasts; and the secession from their native clime, originating from a spirit of enterprize, and not being enforced by hostility, a return was by no means precluded; and the various motives of domestic attachments, of love for the natal spot, and of wants, and of necessities incident to a colony newly fixed in an uncultivated domain, conduced to make the commerce between the new and the mother countries frequent and continued: a knowledge of navigation was thus early introduced into Attica, and the influence it had through every channel, every vein, every the minutest duct of the political body was powerful, and big with consequence.

The practice of navigation so much facilitated the intercourse of distant people, so much therein seemed a public benefit, whilst it conduced to private interest, so much served the enjoyments
of

of the wealthy, and the hopes of all ; that with common voice the powerful purfued fatiety, and the indigent power in the furtherance of every incentive to a general and diffufive commerce.

The pirate and merchant were long fynonimous characters, but good fortune or ability having elevated fome traders to a fuperior eminence in the profeffion, they joined their example, to difcountenance, and power, to quell the violences and depredations of their fellows : it was then, that on the bafis of more general intelligence, of growing wealth and concomitant authority, the merchant's occupation became honorable ;—the ftate reaping fubfidy and population from its practices, modelled itfelf into a fyftem of patronage to its purfuits, and gradually the whole commonwealth became dependant on the fuccefs of its trade, and the prowefs of its navy.

The minds of the Athenians opened by commercial intercourfe, re-operated on that commerce, and aided it with fuch regulation as experience might authorize, or forefight fuggeft : negotiation was to be foftered but by equality, the influence of the citizen over his neighbour might extend to the tranfactions of the merchant,

chant, and diffidence corrode the very root of credit and fair dealing;—thus seemed it necessary, that the state should tend to the democratic scale in subserviency to the interests of those, who gave it grandeur and opulence.

That a state should, by degrees, mould to the spirit of its individuals;—that a humane and impartial legislation tending to favor the occupation of the citizen, should attract the foreigner;—that the public polity should profit of the concourse, and encrease in funds and population;—that industry should lead to riches, and riches to authority;—that each citizen should seek that channel through which his pride, his pleasures, his ambition, his every passion was to be gratified;——that in a word, from the advantages of trade and navigation, a commonwealth should become powerful, and its constituents polished and opulent,——is a subject too well understood, to need any further detail:—but this over-nutritious stimulative to greatness, bears it not somewhat poisonous and destructive in its consequences?—Runs not such a state the career of a midnight revel, progressive through the various steps of civility, wit, and spirit, to the conjoined weakness and hot passion of ebriety;

ebriety; till grown drivelling and torpid, it is oppressed without resistance, and removed at pleasure? In the moral, as in the physical world, the point of maturity is but that of a moment, whilst encrease and decrease have their periods, and in general of reciprocal duration; with the same haste a commercial nation accedes to empire; it speeds to dissolution, and the very circumstances which first opened the prospect of success, prove the cause of its downfall.

Application and frugality the first promoters of trade, finally become victims to the very success of the enterprize; the importation of luxuries gradually enervates the industry that is in pursuit of them; the influx of money at once enhances the value of the manufacture, and renders its artificer indolent; other nations not yet emerged from competency undersell the articles of life;—some subterfuge must be found to evade the rivality,—the liberal arts have perhaps followed commerce to her elevation,—— their assistance is now required,—invention is racked, and workmanship studied of the most exquisite, to allure the sense, and put the comparison of price at a distance;——then too the
mere

mere underling artificer grows idle and moneyed, and puts in his claim with the rest to be dissolute and luxurious:——thus the whole community becomes corrupt, and begins to weigh light in the scale of nations; the last resource from immediate ruin is the restriction of what it actually possesses, to domestic circulation, nor can this preserve it long;—a marine armament is its only defence, and such navy is not to be supported, but on the basis of a commercial one.

Wealth, though the least certain mark of happiness is the surest object of envy; avarice and impatience of inferiority beget emulation and discontent in the neighbouring states; the pride of riches knows not to concede,—a private argument becomes a public quarrel;—war is declared!——the fleets are found on the decline,—the number of artizans is multiplied tenfold, of sailors decreased;—no longer invincible at sea, the commonwealth must have forces too by land;—but whence are they to be drafted? The selfish citizen pleads occupation, the countrymen are but few;—mercenaries must of force be every where collected; still the republic is wealthy, and under hireling banners

banners it opens a campaign at leaft with fplendor;—but thefe troops fight not their own caufe, they are quickly difpirited by lofs, they are mutinous in fuccefs, they are unfupportable to the country, they are exhaufting to the ftate, and whether victorious or not, the war concludes in ruinous debt, and impoverifhed refources.

Such feems the natural career of every commercial ftate dependant on its navy for power and even fubfiftance; without enumerating fortuitous loffes, a defective government, or evil adminiftration; each of which concurred in the prefent crifis, to haften on the republic of Athens in its deftructive courfe, and accelerate the hour of diffolution. The town thronged with flaves, merchants, allies, and foreigners of all forts,—expofed not to immediate view, the ravages which peftilence and war had made in the numbers of the citizens; five thoufand were the moft that ever from this time affembled on the moft general and important concern; but the ftreets wore the appearances of plenty and population, the commonalty were delighted with the view, and maddened with that elation which each demagogue for a private purpofe had artfully wrought up, and now coloured afrefh, with the new Argive treaty,

treaty, they gave ear to every flattery; and filled with the admiration of the speaker and of themselves, harmonized their vanity with his ambition, and accorded to the most extravagant projects of new and extensive conquest.

During the previous contest with the Peloponnese, the Athenians had from time to time meddled in the disputes of Sicily, and relishing the sweets of pillage, which that opulent country afforded, they had become so enamoured with this little secondary war, in which, without hazard, they had acted the profitable part of pyrates, rather than the dangerous one of combatants;—that on the conclusion of the peace at Camarina, they testified their disapprobation of the treaty, by banishing or fining every officer of theirs who had acceded to it: another opportunity now offered of recommencing hostilities there, when despising even appearances, to interpose between the petty states of Selinunte and Egeste, they voted an armament of such mighty force, as could not but be destined for the reduction of the whole country; and made their intentions the more evident, by commissioning their leaders at any rate to pursue the war, and on failure of other pretext

pretext to rip up the old quarrel of Lentini and Syracuse, and make that a pretence for forthwith attacking the capitol of Sicily.

Weakly as this expedition was determined on, more foolish yet was the ordination of the three leaders of the armament—Nicias, a very dilatory, and very old man,——Lamachus, the Lepidus of the triumvirate—and Alcibiades the Antony—equally voluptuous, equally artfull, brave, and unprincipled:—this last man however, was still more improper on other accounts;—previous to the embarkment, he was charged with a crime that was even capital;——without pardon, without trial, or even a determined period of trial, the cause on which his life was to depend, was left undecided, and he was permitted to depart, distrusted by, and distrusting the citizens, and at the head of a soldiery that to a man adored him.

Scarcely landed on the Sicilian shore, Alcibiades was summoned to return, and appear before the assembly, when all who might abet or support him, were absent from the judicature;—but he was aware of the policy of his adversaries,—escaped his conductors, and went over to Sparta:——thus did the Athenians trust this

man

man with power—enter into all his views, and with a vaſt and expenſive force give action to his deſigns,—and then ill uſed, and turned him looſe in the bitterneſs of diſguſt and diſappointment to betray their policy, to counteract their ſchemes, and inſtruct the enemy of what was meant, and what meant to accompliſh it, what was ſtrong, what weak, and where and how his country might be annoyed, and all its projects oppoſed and baffled.

He ſhowed the Spartans, that the Sicilians if conquered, muſt be conquered from want of experience and unanimity—that they had men ſufficient, but that to make theſe men ſoldiers, and bring them properly to the field, they wanted ſome truſty veteran officer to inſtruct, and lead them on. He told the Spartans that their own troops might be more profitably employed in Greece;—that their frequent invaſions of Attica, had not hitherto been ſo effective as they could wiſh; but that the reaſon was obviouſly their omitting, their ſtrangely omitting to fortify and ſecure ſome ſtrong hold in a province, when they were maſters of it, and whence they might at leiſure harraſs the country, intercept parties, and keep the capitol itſelf in conſtant alarm.

The Spartans on their next excurſion, ſtopt

to

to strengthen and garrison the fortress of Decelea, only twelve miles distant from Athens; and immediately they dispatched Gylippus with a small force to inspirit and command the Syracusan armies.

The Athenian armament, of which Nicias now was the sole general, (for Lamachus was killed) was compleatly, and even richly fitted out; its equipment of arms and stores, and its complement of troops seemed adequate to the great business it was sent on;—but at such a distance from home, nothing but constant success could find this army support, and even victory if sharply contested, was fatal, whilst each death was irreparable from the difficulties of recruiting, and the army gradually diminished and wasted away: Nicias indeed sent for succour to Etruria, and even Carthage, but little had his emissaries to plead in favor of their requisition, and they met every where with flight or with reproof.

The Athenians at the first onset were irresistable, they speedily over-ran a large tract of country, seized on Catana, and invested Syracuse: the citizens often sallied forth, and were as often beat; the enemies fleet rode triumphantly in the very harbour; and a circumvallation nearly
surrounded

surrounded the whole town: at this moment of distress, Gylippus arrived, but with so small a force, that even the wary, superstitious old Nicias treated the reinforcement with derision, and no ways labored to prevent the disembarkment; soon however its importance appeared; Gylippus took the lead of the Syracusans, animated them with speeches,——recovered some small forts, elated them with their prowess;—disciplined, formed, and directed them; and finally showed that art and experience could finish the work nature had begun; and that not she, but the military tutor is in fault, if every man is not to be made a soldier.

The Syracusans now often beat the Athenians on equal terms, and the force of the invaders from the successive skirmishes, was so wasted, that not even the reinforcement under Demosthenes could enable it long to make head against the more numerous, and now warlike Sicilians: Demosthenes and Nicias were soon necessitated to act on the defensive;—at length even a retreat was cut off by the blockade of their fleet within the harbour;—they attempted to force a passage, they were repulsed,—the shipping destroyed, and their condition was almost hopeless:

less:—the forlorn alternative was now in agitation, of attempting a retreat by land, and seeking some city, which the Athenian name might yet induce to relieve, and supply them with the means of returning home: the Syracusans aprized of the design, awaited to attack them on their march, they harrassed, they surrounded them, and at length forced them to a discretionary surrender of their arms and persons: Nicias and Demosthenes were put to death;—some were made slaves of, and some dismissed.

Thus concluded this fatal expedition, in which, Ælian says, the Athenians lost forty thousand of their best troops, and a fleet of two hundred and forty sail, ships of war, transports, and others.

C H A P.

CHAP. VI.

CHARITY covers not more sins in religion, than affability in worldly intercourse; an attentive complacency is a refined sort of flattery that none can resist; nor is it wonderful that every man should be in good humour with the possessor of a talent, which puts every man in good humour with himself. There is no one who practises assiduously the art of raising the self-importance of those he may accost, but reaps a good profit in proportion to the dexterity of his address; but extra-advantages have belonged to many both ancient and modern professors of this diffusive and delicate species of practical adulation,—advantages for which they were indebted to the casualties of nature or of fortune, and which no assiduity can hope to emulate;—the man of learning who listens respectfully to a quotation, the man of science to a system, the man of wit to an opinion, and the man of wealth and power who listens respectfully to any thing, will,

will, thereby, give a self-consequence to the speaker, who will heartily repay the donor with a degree of gatitude proportionate to his own unworthiness; which unworthiness, as few have in any extensive sense, learning, science, wit, wealth, or power,—must be the lot of the multitude, and of course, the favor attending the complaisance of the wife, and particularly the great, be much, and almost universal.

From these reflections I have often been induced to take much from the stock of virtues, allowed in great *conciliating* characters, and to return them whence they originated,—on the bounty of mankind; which for every point of lordly dignity given up, is ready to lavish all its powers of eulogy, and elevate to the skies every king who condescends to walk the earth, however lamely he may walk it, with his fellow-creatures.

We hence easily can resolve the wonder of Cornelius Nepos, that Alcibiades exceeded Thrasybulus so much in renown, whilst Thrasybulus was his companion, and accessary to each glorious exploit, and had, besides, engaged in so noble and excentric a one, in which Alcibiades bore no part: Alcibiades, of noble descent, cont, of immoderate wealth, of some wit, and some learning, and much military spirit, was, perhaps, one of those heroes, who have enjoyed many of their more extaordinary qualities from the generous retribution of their cotemporaries; whoever will admire the man whose admiration is creditable, and seems to be placed on them.

Imitation of manners is, perhaps, the most superior sort of this superior flattery;———had Alcibiades eat but one mess of black broath, his austerity would have been noted and enlarged upon at Sparta;———had he uttered two metaphors, and drank two quarts in Persia, his abilities therein, from this small stock might have swelled to a fame, that should rival the hyperboles of the Magi, or the sepulchral inscription of the sot Artaxerxes: I think therefore the versatility of this genius so strongly and so much insisted on, may have been nothing extraordinary, but that merely he had the art, not so common in those days, of polite and assiduous insincerity,

Alcibiades ill repayed the hospitality of Agis, by an adultery with his queen; and this, and other circumstances, obliged him to quit Sparta: at the conclusion of the Sicilian war he

had

had taken refuge with Tisaphernes, and was now ingratiating himself by professing the interests of the Persian, and giving information and advice, ruinous to the liberties of his country: his arguments finally influenced the Satrap to take part in the Grecian disturbances, and to make a treaty with the Spartans, by which they gained a considerable accession of what they so much wanted, and what perhaps alone they had hitherto been deficient in,——money and shipping:——Syracuse too, grateful to her deliverers, listed under their banner, and assisted with her fleets to humble those who had so wantonly been her aggressors.

The total loss of the army in Sicily, the vast preparations making against them, and the successive defection of their allies and tributaries, filled the minds of the Athenians with consternation; every other resource seemed exhausted, and for a last and despondent exertion, they voted the employment of the ten thousand talents set apart for the immediate defence of Athens, and a fleet equipped with its last sad relicts of opulence and authority, again took the seas.

This republic that so little while agone had haughtily menaced the united powers of the Peloponnese

ponnese and Sicily, was now necessitated to secondary expeditions in support of some little town, or for the recovery of some small island, during the attempt on which, another, and another, went over to the enemy, and spite of perseverance, its empire was mutilated, and the strength of each part decayed.

The revolt of Rhodes was announced, that of Eubæa hourly expected;—what comfort, what hopes in this distress! " perhaps, said one, Alcibiades might be persuaded to return; Alcibiades is in strict amity with Tissaphernes, and his interest might bring over the Persian to our assistance: the idea was with eagerness embraced, and the temper and inclinations of his countrymen were immediately hinted to the exiled chief; but now aware of the fluctuating favor of a corrupted populace, Alcibiades would not trust to this momentary good-will; he would return, and boasted he would bring with him all the force of Persia, but it should be on condition that the democracy was abolished, and the government vested in a few, among whom he was to be, and probably to be the chief.

On the promulgation of these proposals, the Athenian assembly broke into a variety of factions,

tions; each adopting such sentiments, party, or plan, as suited with his temper and circumstances; each thinking for himself, and none for the commonwealth. In every other state the intestine commotions being kept up by only two parties; by those who favored the nobles, and those who supported the pretensions of the people, subsided quickly on the superiority of the one or of the other side, and the bloodshed of a few principals washed away the dregs of sedition; but the anarchy of the Athenian assembly admitted not of so easy a settlement: every citizen almost was a party; one man prefered one, and another another form of government; some set up for themselves, and some abetted the pretensions of any one whom they had a little known, or much heard of; many yet stickled for the commonwealth, and a few remembered the old fashioned conduct of their ancestors, said that the duty of a freeman was to bequeath the same freedom to his son; and talked of dying for their liberties and country; but the worst, and not the least numerous set of men were those who without principle or scheme, merely sought to keep up or encrease commotion, with a view of bettering themselves; as

the

the incendiary who first lights, then to pillage from the fire.

A coalition of four hundred of the most powerful citizens, at length with the murder of the few virtuous advocates of the old republic, bore down the other factions, and by a vote dissolving the former compact of government, existed a self-created senate, arbitrary and supreme over every other department, whether civil or military.

To silence the clamours of the discontented, they decreed the adjunction of five thousand more to their number, but this conciliatory promise they never accomplished, and the power was actually and solely vested in the four hundred who had first arrogated authority.

At least a moiety of the Athenian denizens were aboard the fleet at Samos;—those who in the extreme exigency of the republic, had enlisted in its armies, the service of which from the distresses and diminution of the state, was become more frequent and more dangerous, assuredly could not be deemed the worst of the citizens; at any rate military discipline must have given them habits very different from that licentiousness which the turbulency of the assemblies,

blies, the arts of a demagogue, and examples of vice and instances of impunity produced at home;—their dissention from the innovations at Athens was thus to be expected;—and, indeed,—without recurring to more extraordinary reasons than the one so common and so well known,—that they had no part in the transaction, and that men are not generally apt to acquiesce in the work of others, and implicitly approve what they think themselves much concerned and little consulted in.

The army dispatched a messenger to Alcibiades, and putting him at their head, set up for reformers of the commonwealth, in opposition to the faction at home, who had dissolved it: this altercation of army and senate ended in the submission of the latter; their decrees were annulled, and the prior constitution in some measure restored: Alcibiades recalled and supported by the republican party, could not at this time openly propose his favourite oligarchy, but yet apprehensive of that fickleness of disposition he had so much experienced, and had once so nearly fallen a victim to; he was determined to effect such alteration, at least, in the government, as should ensure it to the hands of those,

P. who,

who, from wealth, good fenfe, or other foundation of felf-confequence, might not be expofed to waver to the breath of every noify declaimer, and compliment his oratory with a facrifice of whomever he fhould demand from private envy, diflike, or rivalfhip: Alcibiades had the addrefs to gain his point by ftill preferving the forms of the ancient conftitution, but confining the number of legal citizens to five thoufand, which from his intereft in the choice of the majority of, he thought to make a party of rather than a ftate; and to mold and direct at pleafure.

Courage is generally fuppofed to be conftitutional, or a quality primarily inherent in the connected foul and body; but like all other faculties or virtues beftowed upon us, it is not fo remarkable in the firft inftance, as in the powers we have of encreafing, or adding to it;——as the ftrongeft natural underftanding will yield to a weak one, well taught and well methodized,— or as the beft natural memory will not retain fo well as that of a practifed actor; fo the fierceft fpirit from birth will not act with the intrepidity of a veteran, whom difcipline or ufe, or a particular caufe, or a particular general, or many
other

other casualties will at times induce to face the most eminent peril, with more than natural courage: valour means self-confidence ;—that confidence as it flies from instinct to opinion, not only more easily finds support, but from the conflux of passions flowing in to its aid, that support too is stronger ;—again it is more uncertain whilst the cement of these ascititious emotions is extra-dependant on season and circumstance; and it readily vanishes or returns, as it is urged or repressed by the mind in fluctuation, from reasons of hope, to reasons of fear.

Nothing instills a more undaunted spirit into the breast of soldiers, than an (often most capricious) notion of, and favor for, some particular leader :—with what courage did the name of Charles inspire the Swedes ?—what soldier could shrink, when backed with the clamour of " Cæsar and his fortune ?"--As strong an instance now occurs of military spirit towering to the very heavens from a similar basis, and so idly built, that the fabric was fitted to no other foundation : the name of Alcibiades had caught with the soldiery, and the ardour awakened by the magic of this mere name, inspirited the whole army to that degree, that from their state of

abase-

abasement and humiliation, the Athenians once again assumed the airs of victory,—they won the day at Cynoceme, at Cyzicum, at Byzantium ;——they talked of nought but conquest, and previously to the next defeat of the Spartans, they arrogantly passed a vote to cut off the right hand of every prisoner they should take: with Alcibiades success was not be doubted!—Alcibiades left his fleet with his lieutenant Antiochus;——the hour of engagement was announced,—Alcibiades was wanting;—" Where is our commander?" was asked with an air of anxiety,—the question echoed from vessel to vessel,—the despondency was infectious, every heart drooped;—at the sea-fight off the river Ægos, not a warrior combated with half the nerve or sinew he would have fought, had Alcibiades been present!

The Athenian navy was in this last conflict totally destroyed,—a multitude slain, and three thousand Athenians who were taken, adjudged to death; the plea for this severity was the cruel design adopted of mutilating the Spartan captives, had their enemies been victorious; thus horrid as this massacre seems, it carried an air of justice. The classical reader will hereon

with

with indignation remember, that the *clement* Cæsar practised a similar but more atrocious cruelty on the capture of Uxellodunum, when (as himself tells us) he cut off the right hand of every Gaul who had been guilty of the love of liberty and of his country!

This last overthrow was decisive, and Athens prepared for submission: the Lacedæmonian general Lysander purposely spun out the negotiation respecting the terms of capitulation, till the famine and consequent distress within the town became so great, that the people finally opened their gates, on such conditions as seemed equivalent to a discretionary surrender:—the shipping was to be given up, or destroyed;— the treasury to be at the disposal of the conqueror;—the walls of this noble city to be levelled with the ground;—and lastly, its commonwealth to be subverted, and the odious oligarchy imposed,——the oligarchy which the Athenians so detested, and had spent so much blood and treasure to overturn in every other town of Greece.

Sparta detached a guard to protect the new governors, who moreover bribed to their interest, three thousand of the refuse of the people,

the

the more securely to sport with the lives and property of the rest.

Under the tyranny of thirty of the most rapacious and merciless men that ancient or modern annals have deigned to name, we now behold this once free and flourishing people!—It were easy in fancy to give a lively colouring to a picture of despotic oppression;—let the reader's imagination take up the pencil!—unless he think with me,—that the polish and lenity of the modern age have rendered such subject unnecessary and uninteresting.

CHAP

CHAP. VII.

THOUGH it seems little connected with the historical disquisition I professed to be the subject of my pen, yet am I tempted to introduce into this *already miscellaneous train* of essays some short investigation of the Anabysis of Xenophon.——Xenophon was an Athenian—it is poor excuse for digression!—but it may be no incurious research, to follow the Greeks to Persia, and to mark their conduct and courage in that country whence in former times, invasion came upon them in so monstrous and formidable a shape;—to think of the glorious resistance made to so tremendous an attack by so small a number, and then to consider the fortitude and perseverance of as small a number of the same country, and exerted with similar success in the very centre of that empire which had been the original aggressor.

No where hath Voltaire displayed more levity of criticism, than in his strictures on this expedition;

dition;—shall we say that he was deficient in judgment, or that he wantonly sacrificed it to the vanity of being eccentric, or to a sportive fancy;——when we observe—that he hath rather chosen to descant on the mercenary attack, than on the glorious and indefatigable retreat,—that he hath been a frivolous censurer of a day's march in so stupendous an undertaking, and without argument, and with mere paultry surmise, hath attempted to reprobate the truth of the very writer, who was the very leader of so small a body of men, through so vast a tract of desolate or inhospitable domain;——Voltaire hath justly indeed observed, that Xenophon was never appointed to the command in chief, but we find his advice always given, and as constantly followed, and though not the general, yet may he, not improperly, be termed the leader of the ten thousand.— More singular yet is the Frenchman's account of Cyrus—He lightly talks of him, as of a mere driveling drunkard, notices some obscure anecdotes, and forgets that our author, in the very particular delineation, himself has given of the character of that prince, hath vested him with so bright a series of royal accomplishments, that

that we regard with wonder, the picture so strongly portraited with authentic marks of verity, as to force on us a belief of what almost tranfcends our ideas of excellence, and powers of praife.

When a Spartan army is led forth by a veteran king, flufhed with conqueft, and actuated by refentment, it may be preconceived that fuccefs will await the enterprize, even when directed againft the moft numerous tribes of the populous, but enervate Perfia: I can read of, and yet not wonder at, the victories of Agefilaus.

But that a number of men, collected from diftant parts, driven by misfortune or crime from their paternal hearth, much alienated from patriot fentiments, and long difufed to their national virtues, fhould under the predicament of cafual connexion, recal to mind the focial fpirit and unanimity which diftinguifhed their once loved homes, and form a brotherhood in their diftrefs, faithful in its internal conftitution, and brave and united in its exterior efforts;—that all fhould fo fuddenly lofe fight of mercenary views, and of foreign habits, and in a moment recover the fpirit of old Greece,

and

and assume the deportment of its independant soldiery of yore—all this surely proves how deeply was rooted, and of how pure a nature was the germe of martial virtue born of republican principles and practice,——which no season could corrupt, no difficulties apal, and no time obliviate.

—Cyrus muftered his army at Sardis, and collecting together the Greeks thereof, entrusted them to the generalship of Clearchus the Spartan: in mere sportive evolution this body of men (says Xenophon) displayed a firmness and impetuosity that terrified the spectators, and even army to which they were auxiliary; thence Cyrus had a happy presage of success, and from that moment showed the utmost deference to every soldier of fortune who could plead the merits of a Grecian birth: this favourite band was during the whole tedious march from the coasts of the Ægean to Assyria, enticed, flattered, promised, its wantonness excused, its wildest pretensions heard, and its most extravagant demands acquiesced in;—even when traversing the vast and desolate deserts of Asia, its provision was well supplied, and of good quality, and the famished Persian eyed the Greek soldier

soldier vigorous from plenty, and even ruddy with excess: these circumstances should be remembered when we come to consider them forsaken of prosperity, and yet retaining the elation of spirit, the pride of worth, the contempt of arrogant authority, and all the haughtiness, ease and power could give, and preserving these qualities of the happy, when oppressed by the leaden hand of adverse fortune!

The hostile brothers, Cyrus and Artaxerxes, at length met to enter into decisive conflict for the crown: the Greeks performed the part assigned to them with conduct and courage;—they charged with a fury and discipline that nothing could resist, they broke through whole phalanxes of Asiatics, and were victors on the first onset, with only one man wounded by a random arrow, nor through the whole day of battle did they meet with a vicissitude of superiority, but retired from the field without any loss of consequence to damp the joys of conquest with a tear of regret.

The opposite army consisting of twelve hundred thousand combatants covered a vast extent of ground, and victory on the right, implied no certitude of the general fortune of the day;

the

the Greeks remained under arms the whole night without refreshment, and anxious for the fate of the general; on the next morning came an account of the death of Cyrus, and of the rout and overthrow of all his forces excepting their own, singly-unbroken band; without hesitation the Greeks then sent to the Satrap Ariæus, who was lieutenant to, and had rallied the fugitives, and recovered some remnant of the army of Cyrus; and they offered to support any claim he might make to the Persian diadem; but Ariæus deemed it madness to think of dethroning an hereditary king at the head of more than a million of soldiers, animated with conquest.

Artaxerxes sent to them to deliver up their arms;—we want them (answered Clearchus) whether as friends, or as enemies,—whether to serve him ro to defend ourselves:——they afterwards replied in a haughtier strain, and refused to even treat until supplied with provisions and every other necessary.

The mighty Persian army feared the necessity of coping with the desperation of these few brave men; the refreshment was granted; it was deemed adviseable to substitute treachery

for

for force, and to circumvent, and not to combat with them; nearly were they victims to this mean policy of the Persian, Clearchus and their several other captains being on some amicable pretext allured to the tent of Tissaphernes and there perfidiously put to the sword.

It was now that the virtue and perseverance of the Greeks were put to a hardy trial; those were slain whom habit had taught them to listen to, and to obey; there were none whose long preheminence in council or in action might warrant attention in those around; Xenophon himself was little known among the troops;—" I have heard (said Cherisophus) that one Xenophon an Athenian was with the army, but to the hour of this necessitous debate, I knew not of his particular fortitude and wisdom: the tale of the massacre was unfolded;—the warmth of resentment flushed each private soldier, and with unanimity all breathed the voice of defiance to the cruel and insidious Persian:———the lost captains were immediately replaced with those the most experienced, and most confided in, by the troops; and the firmness of spirit, and national attachment of the soldiery was so great, that distressed and endangered as was this little army,

army of ten thousand men but three hundred Thracians under Miltocythes, and twenty others under one Nicarchus were found base enough to desert their fellow-sufferers and accept the proffers of Artaxerxes. Cleanor (the chief in command) summoned a general council, and the result of the debate, was a determination to force a retreat towards their native country: nor was it in ignorance of its difficulties that they resolved on this expedition;——to induce them to a discretionary submission the rapid rivers, and the mountains and deserts they were to pass, the excesses of climate and famine they were to bear up against, and ferocious nations they were every where, and constantly to cope with,——repeatedly had been urged to them, and the account blackened with every horror the extravagance of eastern eloquence could bestow.

Scarcely had the Greeks struck their tents, when a large detachment under Tissaphernes appeared hovering on their rear; when they began to march, the Persian horse infested them on all sides, they were galled with their darts and javelins, and being without cavalry to pursue, rested in passive torment, the sport of an enemy
wantonly

wantonly brave in the security of his speed: to repel these incursions they gave up their baggage, mounted a choice number of soldiers on the horses; and the next onset, rushing impetuously from within the hollow square, they chaced back the Persian cavalry with confusion from the field. The Persians truly kept them in constant watchfulness, harrassed them with slings and darts, cut off their provender, and intercepted their road;——but it was an enemy they had been so used to conquer, that each soldier was invincible in the confidence built on past experiment; but nature threatened their resolution with a severer trial;———they saw the Tigris pouring a vast and rapid torrent, intercepting their journey to the west; and Northward, whither the only remaining path conducted, appeared the towering mountains of the Carduchi,—a bold and untamed nation, savage in its courage, and of a strength and agility suited to the rugged country it was to defend: Seven whole days were the Greeks in their passage through this inhospitable district, struggling with every obstacle which, from the the face of the country, and belligerant disposi-

tion

tion of its inhabitants, might juſtly be apprehended: rocks were rolled inceſſantly down the precipices, and arrows were ſhot from each covert, of ſuch a length and firmneſs as to ſerve the Greeks inſtead of javelins; and they were ſent from the bow with a force that broke the ſtrongeſt ſhield:——ſuch was the foe they were to combat with, to diſlodge from heights, to break through in paſſes, and every where to fight at odds!

Deſcending from theſe mountains, at the foot, flowed the river Centrites, on the oppoſite bank was a mighty army, and with it a body of the *warlike* Chaldæi, under the Satrap Orontes; and ſtill on their backs poured the arrows of the Carduchi:—but the rich plains of Armenia courted the ſoldier's eye; he was told that the paſſing of this ſtream was his laſt and only difficulty, and that he was to revel in the delightful fields before him, and repay himſelf for every paſt trouble with unreſiſted pillage of the effeminate poſſeſſors. Enured to danger, and enflamed with hope, the Greeks paſſed a rapid and dangerous ſtream, in the face of a numerous enemy, and followed by another, whoſe ſavage force and intrepidity

were

were a match for superior numbers, or for any thing,——save the habitual, cool, valour of discipline, and high spirit of national honor, which made this small body of Greeks so boldly undertake, and so successfully pursue their stupendous design! Having repelled the mountaineers, having crossed the river, having beat the adverse army, having passed beyond the fountain of the Tigris,—other and new dangers awaited them;—Teribazus entered into treaty with, merely to betray them, but they discovered the treacherous design previous to the ambuscade, and revenged themselves with a bloody animosity the perfidy might warrant.

Nor bold nor insidious hostility, nor the natural difficulties accruing from a desert or broken country, had apalled the Greek valour and perseverance;——but from the heavens a fiercer foe came on, and to whom they nearly had yielded;——Winter with all the severities incident to the season in a vast continental tract, threatened them with cold and famine:—continued snows obstructed their march; the constant white glare deprived many of their sight, during the night their bodies were covered with fleakes, isicles hung from their very flesh, their

sandals

sandals were frozen to their feet, and their toes and fingers mortified; many lost the use of their limbs, some had even their senses buried in a general numbness and torpidity, and were only by force of torment brought back to life;—many too died: dearth and cold kept pace together, there was no refreshment to elate the spirits, and fortify the blood against the bite of the frost;—despondency cast a gloom around, and melancholy revibrated from face to face, and from mind to mind,—till all was horror and despair!

——A body of the enemy at this moment approached,—" If we are to die, (said Xenophon) " let us die sword in hand!"——few could be persuaded to follow him; those few, however, were victorious, and animated with success, returned to rouse and encourage their despairing brethren;——they exhorted or compelled them to march, and fortunately soon arriving at some rich villages, the army was preserved: The troops being refreshed, with their strength recovered their wonted fortitude; the small towns to which they were indebted for a few days plentiful support, not being of extent to sustain them for a longer period, they were necessitated to proceed. Other rivers, other sandy plains, other

other mountainous paſſes remained, and other barbarous warriours to defend them; the Chalybes, the Taochi, the Phaſiani, were ſucceſſively worſted, and the whole country, as it were, fought through with unremitting bravery, till about nine thouſand of the thirteen thouſand Greeks who enliſted under Cyrus, arrived on the ſummit of mount Theches, whence diſcovering the Euxine ſea, they rended the air with acclamations of joy! Here they pauſed to ſacrifice to their gods, to recapitulate their troubles, bleſs the divine favor,—and ſomewhat too exult in the courage and conduct which had extricated them from each difficulty.——If ever the ſun ſhone on any multitude, happy without alloy, it was when its ray gilded the armour of the Greeks, contending in the ring, the race, and other ſportive games,—rejoicing in the unwonted celebration. and reminding each other of the appendant uſages in their native Greece,— and what was ſhowy and what neceſſary,—and what might be omitted,—and what was forgotten;——whilſt the view of the ſea gladdened each eye that caſually turned from the ſports, and the anticipation of an eaſy, and no longer toilſome paſſage homewards warranted their mirth, and enhanced the felicity of the ſcene.

Here the retreat may not improperly be concluded, for here its *particular* hardships were at an end: other dangers and difficulties hereafter indeed attended them, but mostly they were the consequence of their own ill conduct; instead of Greeks awakened to fraternal sentiments by the rude call of adversity, we behold men secure, and insolent from success: prosperity quickly transmuted the patriot soldier, into the mutinous mercenary: They divided;—they rejoined, they separated in search of pillage, and whole detachments were cut off; they ordained,——and they deposed their leaders; they entered into alliance, with the Mosynæci; and into service, with Seuthes. *Private* worth may be tutored into excellence by a lesson of misery and ill success, but it too hath other resting place in the natural disposition, and in reason, and in habit;—*public* virtue is the child of, and exists but in adversity:—the flock croud together beneath the storm; and when the day brightens,—separate, and quarrel for a weed!

Whatever superiority may be allowed to the Greeks in every other branch of literature, it cannot be deemed a very hardy assertion to say

that

that in hiftory, they are inferior to the Latins; —the loofe and digreffive tales of Herodotus will bear no comparifon with the firft books of Livy; nor will the more authentic parts of his work relative to the Perfian invafion, raife him to an equal pitch with the writer of the fecond moft memorable decad of the Punic war;— Salluft, rather than Tacitus, I think a proper parallel to Thucydides, and I hefitate not to prefer him over the Greek; nor will the confufed compilations of the Sicilian, nor will Xenophon's fable of Cyrus, or the narrative which he calls his hiftories,——at all affift the Grecian caufe;—Tacitus alone were an hoft againft fuch opponents;—Tacitus, Jopine (and with others I may be permitted an opinion) is the beft of all ancient hiftorians;—nor do I think that D'Avila (perhaps equal to any modern) can well enter into competition with him for the palm.

The military memoirs of Cæfar and of Xenophon may be confidered as a diftinct, and feparate branch of literature, and may afford a new fubject for conteft and for criticifm; the pretenfions of the Roman and of the Greek are refpectively ftrong, and their different merits

may

may afford good subject to the advocate of the one, or of the other language and writer.

I mean not to enter into a minute enquiry; but as a key to such disquisition shall observe, —that in the Latin work, we have the commentaries of a general vested with a legitimate command;—in the Greek, the journal of an officer, chosen by, and dependant on his troops; the speeches of the one, are replete with imperatorial dignity; of the other, delivered with the conciliatory arts of argument and condescension; the oratory put into the mouth of others, is by either author happily introduced, and explanatory with respect to party and circumstance; (with exception however to the speech of Cyrus in the memoirs of Xenophon, who though in quest of the despotic crown of Persia, is made to harangue for Greece and liberty:) accounts of th face of the country, of the characters of the inhabitants, and even of very families were collected, and transmitted to the great leader in chief, and thence from Cæsar we have a curious and well authenticated detail relative to the Gauls, the Britons, and every other enemy;—Xenophon is superficial with respect to any peculiarities of the nations he

passed

paffed through;—his mind was abforbed in the care of thofe under his command,——but thence we are better acquainted with the Greek army, than with that of Cæfar's; Cæfar's attention was ever on thofe he was to attack, to counteract, or to oppofe; Xenophon's on thofe he was to conduct; Cæfar is often very circumftantial, but never diffufe; Xenophon; 'were he lefs eloquent; I fhould call prolix, without being particular; Cæfar gives the characters of men, in a difplay of their actions; and of their speeches; it became not the dignity of the great Roman general, to minutely canvafs the private merits or demerits of an individual;—but Xenophon might properly defcant thereon; with the nice obfervation of a bye-ftander, following the bent of philofophic enquiry; the character of Cyrus were indeed worthy the pen of Cæfar, but a detail of the virtues of Proxenus, and vices of Menon were a more proper fubject for the more private writer: in his portraiture of thefe men, and in that of Clearchus, Xenophon hath fhown the moft nervous and pointed eloquence; the energy of which, is a fine contraft to the eafy rhetoric of the fpeeches, and elegant fimplicity of diction in the narrative

which

which so singularly characterise these most beautiful memoirs. It may be observed, that Xenophon too, hath artfully interspersed every circumstance which might conduce to the giving a favourable idea of his own character;—one Phalinus is introduced deriding him for his virtue and his philosophy;—his happy temper and moderation is hinted at in the observation, that he never had a dispute with any other captain saving once, (and that a trivial one) with Cherisophus; the general idea of his bravery, his religion, and his eloquence is strongly marked throughout;—every speech himself makes (if I rightly remember) is evincive and effectual:—— the τις Ξενοφων Αςηιαιος is thus in succession vested with every accomplishment;. and through the well-wrought veil of modest phrase, is at length discoverable the arrogance of a brave and virtuous, but vain man.

CHAP.

CHAP. VIII.

IS goodness no part of wisdom, that whilst we seek to be wiser, we neglect to be better?— Is it well that the study of virtue is proscribed the schools of philosophy; and philosophy restricted to the experimenter of physics, to the visionary systematic, or to the idle hoarder of shells and prodigies? were it not right whilst we instruct the intellect, to meliorate the mind? —and as we elevate the human understanding, and fit it for serious and deep disquisition, would it not be useful to direct that spirit of research to objects that belong to social humanity,—— to the love of the neighbour, the respect of law, and the adoration of God?——to teach the man the duties of each relative situation, and make him know more, but to the purpose of his more duly fullfilling the end of his being here on earth? Is the academic discourse of no use, but to give food to vanity,—to afford the disciple means of becoming arrogant in learning,

and

and from the very perfection of his accomplishments,—secluded from that philanthropy humanity prescribes,—too proud for that deference society demands,—and disqualified for that humility his religion inculcates?

As the spirit of the enquirists into nature hath soared to the heavens, and left the terrestrial globe less accurately explored;——so do we give up the study of ourselves, for that of the things of the world; and become knowing, in what is known with little use, and surely with much detriment, whilst the hour hath been lightly passed, in which the constitution of reason and passion should have been given its proper habits, and the mind have been, when enlarged, at the same time formed to a moral fitness, under every casualty of season and circumstance.

Are we not ashamed when possessed of the aggregate experience of so many ages, to be less happy in ourselves, and less beneficial to our fellow creatures, than many of less enlightened times?—Are we not doubly ashamed, when with the advantages of a superior moral, and of more authentic rules of conduct, we demean ourselves with less virtue here, and less fortitude on our passage to hereafter,—less virtue in life, and less

fortitude

fortitude in death!——For who of this degenerate age hath lived, or shall die, like Socrates?

The sages of the higher antiquity had been attentive to nature, and some had been visionary, and some subtile;—some had been inquisitive, and had discovered something; and all had been arrogant, and boasted much; they pretended to intuition, rather than to reasoning;—stated an insertion, presumed an hypothesis, delivered a moral apothegm,—and were sanctified to posterity:—but it was not extravagance of fancy, or hardyhood of enquiry, or quaintness of position that seemed laudable in the judgment of Socrates;—" Wander not (said he) into what is fo-
" reign to thy being, but learn to know thyself;
" and to deserve well of those, with whom you
" live, and of him, by whom you were placed
" here on earth."

The memoirs wrote by Xenophon are, perhaps, the most valuable and sterling little work antiquity hath bequeathed us: the pointed particularity of the dialogue, the sentiment, the consistency throughout—all concur to authenticate the relation; and therein, what a portraiture of Socrates! We find him not indeed as in Plato, employed in the investigation of abstract beauty,

or

or other visionary speculation, but we behold him attending to the duties of a good man. Even in the Phædon we have not the character of Socrates rendered aimable and captivating;— ——the manner in which Xantippe is dismissed, and the churlish reproof to Cebes on his presuming to object to a position of his master, show him in the light, of a surly cynic, rather than in that, of a philanthropist modest in his assertions, though confident in his hopes: Xenophon hath given us a picture of the gentle and virtuous friend to mankind; he hath shown him not only establishing a proper sentiment of religion and morality, and laying down principles of what is just and what is good, and what our duty under each known, and each casual relation; but his little offices of humanity too are particularized, and the narrative authenticated by the very names of those, whose distress was alleviated, or vices eradicated by his lessons of prudence and virtue: Lamprocles is gently reproved for his want of filial piety, and induced to ask forgiveness of his mother;—Chærecrates is prevailed on to cherish his brother's virtues, forget his frailties, and bury all unkindness in the tender recollection of the past

joys

joys of fraternal amity;—the good old Eutherus is advised and supported by him; the rich Crito is persuaded to take the poor but honest Archidemus, and to prefer him in his service; and Diodorus is engaged to honour with his friendship, and support the good but penurious Hermogenes; vice he chastises, and folly he derides: he satirizes the fop, and he even condescends to reclaim the *sloven* Epigenes;—every disciple comes from the intercourse a wiser, or a better man.

When the accusation of Melitus was impending over Socrates, and yet he prepared not any written or studied defence;——" wherefore (said Hermogenes) do you trifle away the precious hour in desultory discourse, and not think of some answer to the arguments of your accuser, or some plea to the favor of your judges? —" that answer (replied Socrates) hath been the business of my whole life,——of a long life throughout, strictly conformable to justice and piety!"—to this idea he firmly adhered, confided in his virtue, and submitted to the event with a resignation which could proceed from nought but a sound faith in the being and goodness of the great and ever * super-intending God.

Though

* Θεος επιμελουμενος. Plat. Phædd.

Though the dialogue with Crito probably never passed, yet the offer of Crito was probably made;——though the long detail of Phædon to Echecrates is doubtlessly not authentic with respect to the argumentative part, (for nor was Plato present, nor could even Plato (if present) have classed and related at second hand so prolix and subtile a course of argument) yet is the essay in many parts curious from the anecdotes interspersed, and through the notoriety of which, Plato probably thought to give a genuine stamp to the philosophical parts of his treatise:—among these may be remarked—'the observation of Socrates with respect to pleasure and pain, when his fetters were knocked off;'—'his versification of the fable of Æsop;'—'the sacrifice to Æsculapius,' and many other circumstances, among which ought never to be forgotten, the kind smile and blessing he bestowed on his executioner, whose lowering eye could not refrain a tear, when he held forth the deadly cup to so good and wise a man.

"To me (exclaims Xenophon) his death
"itself seems a demonstration of how much he
"was beloved of the Gods! who cut off the
"few remaining burthensome hours of life,
"and

"and on the eve of decrepitude, granted him
"the easiest of deaths!

"Such was the wisdom, and such the mag-
"nanimity of this man, that I ever must re-
"member, and remembering, ever laud it;
"and if, in future times, any who are friends
"to virtue, and to the virtuous shall boast ac-
"quaintance with a better and with a more
"*useful* member of society, than was Socrates,
"—I hesitate not to pronounce him the first
"and most blest of mortals.

CHAP.

CHAP. IX.

IN the prior times of the republic, in order to speak impartially, I spoke but little of individuals;—nay,—I testified my disapprobation of the writer who should degrade a community, by a selected instance,—and drawing the attention of his reader from the characteristcs of a great nation, to the character of a great man, seem to bid him remark transcendant virtue as an exception, and not a rule:—respecting those times, I think I was right;—the whole people during the Persian wars, seemed so united in their pursuit of what was good, and what was great, that to praise one, seemed injustice to all;—but this galaxy of bright and excellent qualities, wherein to distinguish, and fix on, any one more bright and more excellent than the rest, was so difficult for the eye, gradually lost its indiscriminate lustre, and became a constellation of lesser and of greater stars, which in proportion to the dimness of the whole, have shone out conspicuous to the view, and have

attracted

attracted our attention to their preheminence:—thus my regard (I perceive) hath of late unwarily been drawn from a confideration of the whole, to its more particular and luminous fpots: looking back on my comment, I find it from time to time, attending more and more to individual names and to characters;—the further I proceed, the more, I forefee, I fhall thus deviate from the principle I at firft laid down;—but this deviation, originates it not in the progreffive, and inevitably changeable courfe of my fubject?

We left Athens to rue its paft crimes and follies under the tyranny of the Oligarchy; cruelty and oppreffion had foon profcribed or driven into exile the beft of the citizens; and fcattered through the neighbouring ftates, they were idly bewailing their lofs of the country:——" In thefe times, fays Nepos, (and I think he might have faid it of all times)—good men were more inclinable to harangue, than to fight for liberty:" fuch converfation however is not without its confequence; the mind is thereby moved from its paffive ftate, and may thence forward be more eafily directed to a particular action, if there is any one to impel or lead it on.

R   Thrafybulus,

Thrasybulus, a captain of some renown in the latter period of the Peloponnesian war, was among those who had taken refuge in Thebes;—(for Thebes and every other state of importance was willing to receive and cherish the Athenian fugitives) the extirpation of a people who had so long balanced the empire of Greece, seemed a prelude to the uncontroulable dominion of the opposite party; the apprehension of any further encroachments of Sparta gained favor to those who alone had seemed equal to the opposing her pretensions;—thus others, besides its banished citizens, wished, and some were ready to abet, the restoration of the republic, and once again set it up in hostile rivalship to the power of the Peloponnese.

The temper of men was in that state, that nothing but a first mover seemed wanting;— Thrasybulus had the dexterity to engage, and courage to lead forth seventy followers on a sudden and desperate expedition; and the first wheel being thus touched, the whole machine was quickly in motion: this small party issuing out in the depth of winter, surprized a fortress in the vicinity of Athens, from the severity of the season, not strictly guarded or attended to;
—the

—the fame of fuccefs encreafed their numbers; —they marched on to the Piræeus:——feized Munychia;—met, and defeated the mercenary forces of the Oligarchy;—flew two of the chiefs, and clofely laid feige to the remainder, who diftrufting their venal army fent for fuccour to Lacedæmon.

The incertitude and vanity of our moft general and favourite maxims, appears on every refearch into, and long inveftigation of fucceffive and dependant events:——what opinion appears fo inconteftable, as that the variance of leading men, whether of ftate or army, is of the moft fatal tendency to thofe under their command! Lyfander fet out with an adequate force to repel the party of Thrafybulus, and replace the Oligarchy in a firmer, and more defpotic fovereignty; Paufanias the king of Sparta, envied the renown, and feared the growing authority of Lyfander, and going forth, as he pretended, to reinforce, and affift the prior detachment, he took the lead in the expedition, and from defire of counteracting, and vexing his rival, withheld the fword, treated with the exiles, and permitted the reinftation of the commonwealth. —What Spartan at that period did not think the interests of his country betrayed by the animosity of the generals?—but posterity observes, —within a few years from the epoch, when the state of Sparta was borne down, and menaced with utter destruction by the Theban, that it owed its safety to the interposition of Athens, —whose power to save, and good will to interpose,——had never been, but for the dissentions of Pausanias and Lysander!

The republic was now, like a convalescent, purged indeed of many gross and noxious humours, but as yet of a weak and tremulous frame; adversity, that best preceptor, had bestowed no unprofitable lesson; penury had broken the habits of dissipation, and danger, and the heavy hand of poverty, had enured the courage, and humbled the arrogance of the citizens; they sat out anew without partialities for any demagogue to lead them astray, and without wealth to corrupt them; but then, their former empire was mutilated, or rather gone; their arms,—their very shipping was destroyed, and they had nought to trust to for their elevation, but the never failing, and enegic spirit of their government,—the *genius of the democracy!*——this however could not be

the

the work of a moment:—the first we hear of the Athenians, after the expulsion of the Oligarchy; is, that they followed the Spartan, an humble and dependant ally to the Elean war.

Leotychides, the son of the queen Timæa, was suspected to be the fruit of her intimacy with Alcibiades, and with the help of a few oracles newly vamped up, and well explained, was illegitimated in favor of his uncle Agesilaus; who conscious of the doubtful right by which he held the crown, sought by an animated conduct, to draw the attention of men from his title, to his merits; and make not, *why*,——but *how*——he wielded the sceptre of Sparta, the scope of observation: Lysander had anticipated the crop of laurels from Greece; but Asia seemed a fresh and inexhaustible field of renown; and thither he directed the war. The Satraps in the maritime governments of Persia, desirous of diverting the storm, sent forth emissaries to intrigue with every Grecian city of importance, and to incite them to hostilities with Sparta: It was a favorable crisis for shaking off the dominion of that haughty state;—a rupture was pleaded for with all the force of oratory, and that oratory backed with more persuasive gold:

Thebes,

Thebes, and many other states received the advice and money of Persia with approbation; Athens had at this period re-adopted some notions of the patriot virtues of her ancestry, and admitted not the arch-briber of Rhodes within her walls; but the opportunity of raising herself, with all Asia, as it were, to help her, and in her turn to set her foot on the neck of those who had treated her so harshly in her moment of distress, flattered too much her ambitious hopes, and ardour for revenge, for her to resist the invitation: an honorable pretext for intermeddling was easily found;—Thebes had opened her gates to the Athenians in exile, and the Athenians from gratitude voted an offensive and defensive alliance with Thebes, who was connected offensively and defensively with the Persian.

Various other states were bribed or persuaded into similar measures, till the social league became of so great extent, and importance, that Sparta, to oppose its progress, was necessitated to recall its troops from Asia; Agesilaus with regret obeyed the summons;——he had done enough to irritate the king of Persia, and had not done enough to benefit the cause of his country;

country;—he had merely made, and left an enemy;—and his expedition had the effect of a miniſtry, to conciliate the Aſiatics with Athens; rather than that of an armament, to humble them to Sparta.

Conon profited of the juncture to connect himſelf with Pharnabazus; he had not ſeen his country ſince the reſtoration of the democracy; his behaviour in the laſt ſea-fight with Lyſander, had rendered his integrity or courage ſuſpected, and under theſe circumſtances he thought proper to delay his return, till a favorable opportunity ſhould occur, of recovering the good favor of the people, and reviſiting his natal ſpot with advantage and glory; he had ſo far ingratiated himſelf with Pharnabazus, that he entruſted him with the command of the Ionian, and other provincial detachments of the Perſian fleet; off the city Cnidus, a city of the Carian Doris, nearly oppoſite to Rhodes, lay the united naval force of the Spartans; Conon came up with, attacked, defeated, and deſtroyed, or diſabled the beſt of the ſhipping;——Honor once again took poſt by the Athenian flag, and Fame again trumpeted from the prow, the ſtories of Mycale and of Salamis.

On

On land too the republic was once more taught to vaunt the prowess of its soldiery, under the generalship of Iphicrates: Seven and twenty long years of almost continued civil war, had shown that mere Herculean force might be counteracted by dexterity,—that, in a word, there were *arts of war*; and this ingenious people seem to be the first who turned this, as well as every other art, to its proper account. Iphicrates had so disciplined, so armed, and so instructed every soldier of his army, that the citizen who had seen service under his command was valued thereon, and thereafter received an advanced pay, under the title of an Iphicratensis: Chabrias too was another great master of evolution, and every other military science, and once in this war, by a simple, new, and unexpected manœuvre, put a stop to the career of Agesilaus at the head of the whole Spartan army, elated with victory, and in the heat of pursuit.

The Athenians, under these generals, were dailily gaining ground: when in company with their allies, they had, indeed, been beaten by Dercyllidas; but in separate detachment had under their skilful leaders, every where met with success; they had been victorious in the countries

tries of Arcadia, and of the Phliafii, and they had furprized and put to the fword a large body of Spartans at Lychæum.

Conon arriving with the money and fleets of Perfia at this period rebuilt the walls of Athens; from that moment Sparta ceded fomewhat of her pretenfions, and condefcended to treat on equal and equitable terms: after much negotiation the general peace called that of Antalcidas took place; and Perfia, the Peloponnefe, and its oppofites, univerfally agreed to conditions of amity, never long, or much attended to.

The weight of the fierce, and almoft continued, civil broil in Greece had fallen moft heavily on Sparta and Athens, and on fuch petty cities as were not of fufficient confequence to be treated with deference and care by the great mafter-republics: another, an intervening rank of ftates, whofe alliance was fufficiently important to exact confideration, and whofe ftrength was fuch as to enfure fafe and honorable capitulations—fuch fattened on the war; and as the expence of wealth and men gradually weakened and impoverifhed the contending and principal parties, thefe fecondary republics fucceflively ftarted up, and each a

while

while figured on the theatre of history in some chief and leading part.

Olynthus in Thrace was among those which had grown so heavy of late in the balance of sovereignty; all the cities of the vicinity were within its jurisdiction; and Amyntas complained to Greece, that half his Macedonia and even its capitol Pella, had yielded to the forces or intrigues of this encroaching neighbour: A considerable army was sent from Sparta under the conduct of Eudamidas, to equipoize the scale of power in those parts;—this he effected;—but scarcely was this new excrescence lopt, when from the very blow another hydra-head shot forth, and breathed defiance, and even menaced destruction to the assailant.

Phæbidas in his march to reinforce Eudamidas in Thrace, stopt on his way to profit of a commotion in Thebes and assist and establish the oligarchic party, and he left a detatchment to protect the usurpation. The enterprize of Pelopidas, who surprized and massacred the Spartan guard, recovered the citadel, and restored the commonwealth,—embroiled his country with the lordly conquerors of Athens;—unexpectedly it proved equal to the conquest; and Sparta, in

her

he turn was to tremble for her dominion, for her country, for her very safety, and even existence.

The Athenians were desirous of setting quiet spectators of the contention, but the foolish outrage of Sphodrias who treacherously but vainly made an attack on the haven of Athens, infringing the treaty with the Lacedæmonian forced the Athenians into a separate treaty with Thebes, and they prepared to join in a vigorous attack on the common aggressor.

Now once again, a fleet was equipped from the Piræeus; Chabrias and Timotheus its commanders were every where successful; the one drove the enemy from the seas, the latter recovered Samos and took Corcyra, and coasting the peninsula, at various descents despoiled its cities and laid waste the country.

The Theban however reaping all the advantages of the war, and throwing more than the proportional weight thereof on the allies, Athens in disgust seemed inclinable to treat, and giving up a contest which she had entered into but from necessity, to recur to a tranquil pursuit of population, of arts, and of the recovery of that commerce which had once rendered her so rich

and

and powerful: Iphicrates was recalled from Acarnania, where he was dailily acquiring credit and advantage, and a treaty was commenced and separate conditions of peace agreed to between Athens and Sparta.

Thebes left alone to prosecute the war, was for a time dispirited, till in the field of Leuctra, that great and (more than great that) good citizen Epaminondas by a sage and valiant conduct routed and compleatly vanquished the Spartans with an army less numerous than their own;—elated with so noble a victory over a people used to despise all odds, and ask——*not how many, but, where their enemy were,*—crowned with so bright a conquest, the Theban proclaimed it with exultation throughout Greece, and invited each city to partake in the humiliation of the haughty disciples of Lycurgus, and join in the abasement of those who had so long and so tyrannically played the lord and master. Athens gave the herald of success but a cool reception: it was matter of debate, not whether Sparta should be attacked, but whether Thebes opposed; the dismemberment of Sparta and accession of its territories to Thebes, so much encreasing its power, might swell the current,

rent, already full to its bank, till it burſt in inundation over the vicinities, and lay all around under the flood; it ſeemed time to draw off ſome of the ſtream, or at leaſt to place a dam to its further encroachment; Athens had already beheld the power of Sparta ſpread over her countries, and over the face of Greece, and not even with the deſtruction of Sparta would ſhe hazard from another quarter ſuch another deſolation of the liberties, of the arts, of the free intercourſe, and of every other bleſſing of ſociety ſ In a full aſſembly, it was concluded neceſſary to obviate the growing power of Thebes, and now when no other city was willing to engage in ſo diſtreſsful an alliance Athens voluntarily profered friendſhip and ſuccour to the Lacedæmonians, and Iphicrates accordingly was ſent forth with an army to their aſſiſtance.

Not long after, in the famous battle of Mantinea with the heroe Epaminondas fell the greatneſs of his newly ambitious countrymen: The Thebans, by the advice of their dying general forewent the hopes of empire for a well timed and honorable peace which generally was come into, and with a particular readineſs by Athens, as the equal power and freedom ſhe
fought

fought for, seemed virtually secured by the very armistice.

Each great and leading state of Greece had, in its turn, known the vicissitude from power to humiliation, each had dearly rued a short-lived triumph with the loss of its treasure, and of the flower of its citizens; every speech abhorent of war, was echoed by the groans of the widow or the orphan; the peace might now, therefore, be presumed permanent, whilst the public ruin and private misfortunes gave every argument for it, its full weight, and a most favorable hearing. Peace, however, like a feast long untasted, and then gluttoned on to excess, brought on gross corruption, and a whole train of disorders: Men, because disgusted with war, seemed to think that their service in war was never again to be required; they gave themselves up to habits that incapacitated them for future labor; the fund set apart to any unforseen exigencies of the public, was voted for public dissipation, and their late brave and succesful generals, disregarded by the people, and carped at by the demagogues, fled from envy and disgrace, and settled in distant parts;—Conon in Cyprus, Iphicrates in Thrace, Timotheus at Lesbos,

Lesbos, and Chares in Sigæum. Little was it considered that a warlike mien, and an attentive and firm policy were the best sureties for the continuance of that state of tranquillity so much and so ill enjoyed: the rest of Greece seemed too much enraptured with the same indolence, or too much exhausted to attend and profit of the weakness which supineness or luxury should produce among others; and it was not pre-conceived that a petty northern prince might, as he did, break through the obstacles that opposed him, and come with a force irresistable to the enervate Grecians, and in a short time attain that sovereignty, which had so long and so sharply been contested.

Our Athens was in particular lulled into the most supine security; attack was so little thought of, that every provision for even defence was diverted to some other channel; their generals, as we observed, lived in a sort of voluntary exile; their army and shipping were left to wreck and ruin, and the funds applicable to their support, wasted on scenery and actors.

Nor were other great cities less votaries of corruptive ease;--nor was even Sparta without infection;--Lysander had brought home the gold of
Persia,

Persia, and spoils of Athens;—Antalcidas their ambassador to Persia, on the late peace, to divert the great king, danced a saraband,—and buffooned the heroism of Leonidas.—Can we wonder at the successes of Philip!

CHAP.

CHAP. XI.

THE people of Athens, from the inactivity of the neighbouring states, drew a false conclusion favorable at once to their love of ease, and to their ambition of power: as the the moment of ebriety gives a transitory force, and even to the worn-out rake affords a sensation of vigour not much dissimilar to that of a robust and healthful constitution, or if discriminate, yet differing only in a show of superior heat and impetuosity; so, the Athenians inflated with luxurious and unmolested enjoyment, assumed the haughty deportment of high and invincible authority, and treated their dependants with such indignity and oppression, as drove them to a defiance, and to a trial of that force which had so wantonly been exercised upon them, whilst in passive submission.

The city of Byzantium, and isles of Chios, Cos, Rhodes, and various other places, conspired to humble the arrogance, and prescribe some limits to the jurisdiction, of the sovereign republic: this, commonly called the social war, was but of short duration; Chares sent to chastise the islands, transgressed the authority of his commission, by making a descent on the coasts of Ionia, and assisting the rebel Satrap Artabazus, against the king of Persia; who irritated by the unprovoked attack, menaced Attica, with an invasion, the more formidable, as it was at this period at variance with the better, namely with the naval, part of its common tributaries: the threats of the Persian king brought on an immediate treaty between Athens and its dependencies, and the peace soon after concluded, gave them unprecedented rights and privileges, established on the necessities and fears of the master-state.

Other circumstances too influenced the Athenians to put an end to this war at any rate; Chabrias, their most experienced commander, had fallen at the attack of Chios; and the designs of Philip hitherto conducted with the most wary policy, and covered with every art of intrigue and negotiation, were now sufficiently opening to view, for even the blindest to have some glimmering of the scope to which they directed,

rected, and some apprehension of the ruin that must ensue: Athens more particularly had reason to take alarm; some of the few relicts of her once powerful empire were scattered on the confines of Macedon, and its kings first object was the seizure of these several frontiers of his dominion, to secure, as well as to enlarge his own territories, previous to an avowal of his more ambitious purposes; unfortunately it might have turned out for him, that many of these barrier towns were appendant to the sovereignty of Athens;——unfortunately I say,—— for had that degenerate state, instead of seeking arguments for its lascivious indolence, been maturely watchful over the motions of Philip; awakened by his attack on its own particular rights had it interposed, and given a timely support to its cities; or *at first*, had it accepted the proffered alliance of Olynthus, this plotting monarch checked on his first outset, had not thenceforward dared to meditate his extensive schemes of conquest and command. The Athenians amused and lulled into a fond security by the intrigues of Philip, and soothed by his protestations at the very time he was mutilating their empire, and undermining their dearest interests, are a curious instance, of in how short a time a vicious luxury can abase the understanding as well as spirit of a brave and enlightened people!

Amphipolis was one of those cities which Athens had lost during the Peloponnesian war, and which from the close of that contest, had refused to recognize its pretensions; with the repossession of this city Philip still soothed and cajoled them; he promised it them in exchange for Pydna, and they rejected the friendship of the Olynthians; he himself then entered into a compact with the Olynthians, and seizing Pydna, and Potidæa, made a present of them to his new allies; still he found means to conciliate the Athenian assembly;——finally he invested Amphipolis, and had the address to persuade the people, or rather they had the stupidity to be persuaded, that the expence and dangers of this siege, were incurred merely on their account, and that the fruits of its success were to be theirs: his attack at length on the Chersonese admitted not of prevarication; and Chares with a small force was sent to oppose his progress in those parts; Cersobleptes the rightful sovereign, gave up his pretensions thereto, in favor of Athens;

thens; but Cardia its capitol, hoifted on its citadel the enfigns of Philip, who having worfted Argæus, his competitor for the throne of Macedon, and having been victorious in Illyria, in Theffaly, and in Thrace, doubted not with this footing place in the Cherfonefe, of foon maftering too the reft of that peninfula.

Methone was befieged by this enterprizing and politic warriour;——Athens debated,—and voted affiftance;——the time fpent in debate fhould have been the hour of action; the affiftance came,—but it came too late.

Pagazæ was invefted;—again Athens voted fuccour;—and again from its dilatory progrefs, that fuccour was fruitlefs.

An account arrived, that Heræum, the key to the city of Byzantium, whence their commercial riches, whence their very neceffaries and and provifions flowed, was attacked and reduced to the laft extremity;—the Athenians in the utmoft alarm, voted fubfidy, ordered levies, and ——on the news of Philip's falling fick, countermanded thofe fubfidies and thofe levies, and fell back in their priftine lethargy.

However flattering the munificence of Philip had been to the Olynthians, that people could

not,

not, without apprehenfion, behold this growing power, ftep by ftep, encircling their whole territory; their immunities feemed dependant on his generofity,—their very city, exifting from mere fufferance: it was deemed fitting in time to fecure fome potent and interefted ally to obviate the danger, which the now confpicuous ambition of their encroaching neighbours feemed to warn them of the approach of; Philip apprized of their policy, anticipated the attack, with a declaration--" That he would have Olynthus, or lofe Macedon :"— to Athens this people then a fecond time fent an embaffy, to proffer their friendfhip, to plead their common interefts, and roufe the people to a juft fenfe of their own loffes, and future danger——" * Well, (faid Demofthenes) there is
" no

* Of late it hath been as ufual to load a work with authorities, as a minifter with credentials;—a cuftom I never could fee the ufe of, (except to catch the eye)—for thofe who are deeply learned, will readily difcover the error, ignorance, or falfification of the author, and thofe who are not, would be little wifer, were the margin to be crouded with a whole claffic catalogue. In this chapter, however, I have pointed out the *fparfim excerpta* from Demofthenes, as the reader defirous of recurring to the beauties of the original, might have fome trouble from the

paf-

" no further excuse for procrastinating the pub-
" lic weal;—long,—long have ye murmured;
" oh that the Olynthians were but detached from
" Philip! the very event hath occurred;—— *Paris*
" nay, even exceeded your fondest wishes; for 1570.
" Ολυνθ.
" had they taken up arms at our instigation, sect. 9
" they would have been,——(they themselves
" know it) they would have been but wavering
" allies; but since it is inveteracy rooted in
" their own dissatisfactions, which engages them
" in this war, the compact with us will be the
" more firm, as strengthened by their own
" private sufferings or apprehensions.————
" ——————If he shall meet with un-
" interrupted success, what is to prevent his lead-
" ing his forces into Greece? The Thebans!
" —(pardon the severity of the thought) they Id. sect.
" will rather assist him;—but the Phocians!— 35.
" a nation which for its security, its very exis-
" tence is dependant on your friendship and pro-
" tection.—Some other alliance!—or perhaps
" he will not make the attempt?—oh most ab-
" surd,—that the intention which even in incer-
                                        " titude,

passages being quotted with so little regard to order,—even
those of the same oration.

" titude, he manifests ; in power, he should not
" execute !"

To alarm the Athenians into an early and expeditious vigilance, with what force doth the orator follow the velocity of their enemy's career?—" Consider, O Athenians, from what an
" humble and insignificant state, Philip hath ari-
" sen to this pitch of greatness!—It was first
" seizing Amphipolis, afterwards Potidæa and
" Methone;—then turning to Thessaly, he
" over ran the counties of Phera, of Pagasæ,
" and Magnesia;—thence rushing into Thrace,
" he subverted some, he exalted other states;—
" he fell sick;—scarcely convalescent, he left
" not his sword a moment to rust in sloth, but
" wielded it against Olynthus : I have not men-
" tioned his expeditions against the Illryrians,
" the Pæonians, and Arymbæ;—and indeed
" where have they not essayed !"

This speech had weight with the assembly, and they determined on an immediate aid to Olynthus; which, according to the usual fate of their decrees was too late for its purpose, and Philip got possession of the town and leveled its walls with the ground: the military levies however were not without their use ; they served to

keep

sect. 19.

keep up a balance in Eubæa, whither Philip's intrigues had already penetrated; and they retarded the Macedonians entrance into Greece, giving him a timely repulse at the straits of Thermopylæ.

I mean not in the quotations I may make from the orations of Demosthemes to give a just idea of the spirit and energy of his eloquence, or of the art and cautious skill with which he curbs or directs its seemingly wild and impetuous course,— like an Alexander making docile his fiery Bucephalus: the rhetoric of Demosthenes, no more than the poetry of Pindar, is to be known from modern translation; but the present temper of the people whose genius and history I investigate, are no where so strongly marked as in the speeches of this orator,—and to an elucidation of this subject I employ the subsequent extracts.

The rich and poorer men of the state may be supposed combating with all the virulence of arrogance and envy—" I think (says Demost-
" henes) it may be of some service to the commu-
" nity, to plead the cause of the wealthier against
" the meaner denizons, and reciprocally that of the
" poorer against the rich:"—we find the opulent avariciously witholding the dues of the common-

mon-wealth;—"at a time that the annual tri-
"butes of this state amounted but to one hun-
"dred and thirty talents, no one whose income
"was adequate to the charge, refused the ex-
"pence of Trierarch; the vessels were properly
"fitted out;—the monies paid in;—every office
"discharged: enriched, as is now the republic,
"shall we set blaming and bickering at one ano-
"ther, and in our very quarrels seek and plead
"excuse for procrastinating our payments and
"neglecting our duty?" We then behold the
populace rapacious and inflamed against the
rich;—" the balance of the common-wealth
"(continues the orator) is to be duly and equably
"held; as the wealthier part of the people con-
"tribute much, and hazard most, in the exigen-
"cies of the state, so are they entitled under its
"shelter to unmolested possession of what is
"justly theirs; and, as what justly may be
"demanded by the community, they have no
"right to retain; so, on the residue of their pro-
"perty none have a right to trespass."

How evident is the degradation of the common-wealth, when we hear that—" neither to Me-
"non the Pharsalian who had given a volunta-
"ry succour to the state of twelve talents, and
"had joined their army with two hundred horse-
men;

" men; nor even to Perdiccas the king of Ma-
" cedon who aided to destroy the Persians at
" Platæa,—in reward for such generous service
" did our ancestors decree the full rights of citi-
" zenship, but deemed them sufficiently honored,
" when admitted to a mere freedom of their
" city;—the name of their then virtuous and
" enobled country, they thought a gift tran-
" scending the most exalted merits or services!—
" but *now*, O Athenians, we make citizens of the
" most abject and profligate,—of very slaves,
" born in servitude,—of all, who can buy our
" franchisement—put up to sale, like a mere
" and common vendible."—And in another
oration,—" from the very meanest stocks have
" suddenly arisen men who eclipse our most re-
" nowned, and opulent families; they have
" houses that tower above our public edifices;
" and the more ruinous the condition of the re-
" public, the more flourishing seems theirs.—
" whence comes all this?—whence the differ-
" ence between these times and those of yore?—
" when the citizens themselves boldly went forth
" to war, they had a consequence which ren-
" dered them lords over their own magi-
" stracies; what properly *should* be, *was* under
                                       " their

Oλυνϑ. γ.
sect. 40
1-2.

"their controul, and the candidates condefcend-
"ed to receive all office, and all honours, at
"their hands and option;—*now*, the magiftrates,
"independant mafters of your wealth and pow-
"er, tranfact all bufinefs as their own; and ye,—
"an enervate people—crouch to them like fer-
"vants, for your pay, and thank them if they
"allow ye (what is your own)— a paltry ftipend
"wherewith to bask it in the theater!" How
pathetically doth the fpeaker than remark the
declenfion of the grandeur of Athens concomitant to the depredation of its citizens!—"A no-
"ble harbour, temples, edifices, every ornament
"that could enoble this city we have, bequeath-
"ed to us by our anceftors, and of a magnifi-
"cence which pofterity hath by no means rival-
"ed;—look yonder at that naval key,—that
"Portico,—and thofe ftructures all around ye!
"but *then* the private houfes of the moft illuf-
"trious citizens correfponded with the equa-
"lity which is the boaft of our conftitution; let
"any one find out the houfe of Themiftocles,
"of Cymon, of Ariftides, or of Miltiades,—
"it is not better than his neighbours; — *now*
"we think it enough, to mend a road, direct
"a water fpout, incruft a wall, or to effect
                                        "fome

" some equally trivial work;—but from the pu-
" blic pillage many have built them houses
" that o'ertop our noblest temples."

The reader will naturally suppose that a luxurious people may be proud, though indolent, and talk highly though act meanly:——
" Whenever (says Demosthenes) your debates
" comprize those particulars wherein Philip hath
" infringed his engagements, I observe every
" oration to appear candid and equitable,—
" every speaker to seem sagacious and perti-
" nent, in proportion to his allegations and ran-
" cour against Philip;—yet no consequent acti-
" on,—no efficacy marking the utility of such
" discourse!"

Φιλιππ. 6 sect. 1.

The few spirited decrees they made,—how tardy the execution thereof! says our orator—
" If you hear Philip is in the Chersonese, you con-
" sider—and sent a reinforcement to the Cherso-
" nese;—is he at Pylæ? Why then the army is to be
" sent to Pylæ;—or any where else?—this way or
" that way ye are after him, following him as
" if ye were his mercenaries, rather than his
" enemy.————Philip is fallen sick!—or
" Philip is dead!—It would signify not; your
" present idleness and vices would soon raise
" another Philip; for it is not from his own in-
"   trinsic

Φιλιππ. sect. 55.

Φιλιππ. sect. 16

" trinsic strength and means, but from your su-
" pine weakness that this man is become so
" great."

Those who act not when they ought, will of course envy the success and cry down the merit of those whose vigorous and timely exertion brings shame on their indolence; this observation is verified from the oration in defence of Diopithes, who had attack'd the rebel cities of the Chersonese.—" We neither contribute to the public
" exigencies, nor enter on military service, nor
" even abstain from diverting to improper uses the
" funds of the republic; — but we can abstain
" from affording due subsidies to Diopithes, or
" from the praise which his diligence hath me-
" rited; we can cavil at his exploits, and en-
" viously blame his past, or idly speculate on
" his future conduct."

Like an overheated drunkard the state was vain-glorious and conceited, and to humiliate and bring the people to a proper sense of their perilous situation, we observe this sage counsellor in various passages, and particularly in the first Olynthiac above-cited, raising their fears and humbling their arrogance; but the vitiated temper of this people was, as might be pre-conceived, subject

to viciſſitudes of terror and deſpondency;—we find the orator, in his ſecond Olynthiac, flattering and conſoling them, depreciating every reſource of Macedon, and every great quality of its king:—of all paſt virtues, their repreſentative pride was the only relict to which he could make an effectual appeal; his oratory therefore teems with references to the exploits of their anceſtry, and with remembrance of their former empire and ſpirit;--" Philip (ſays he) will never be ſa-
" tisfied with ſubduing,—he muſt deſtroy,—he
" muſt ſubvert the very foundations of this city;
" for he knows that ye could not endure a ſtate
" of ſervitude; or if ye would, that ye could
" not;—for ye have ever been accuſtomed to
" command:" the ſhame too the Athenians will incur throughout Greece is likewiſe painted in animated colours;——nor this,——nor every other argument,——nor the remonſtrances he made uſe of,—nor even a recapitulation of the juſtice of his paſt reaſoning and predictions could recover the aſſembly from its blindneſs, its indolence, its avarice, and general depravity.

Ολυνθ. α. Φιλ. γ. &c. ſparſim.

περι των εν χερρονησω ſect. 81.

περι το εν χερρον. ſect. 62.

περι ειρηνης ſect. 5. & ſeq.

The above tranſlations from Demoſthenes I have adduced to prepare the reader,--for the ſubverſion of all that has rendered the hiſtory of this republic

republic so interesting to our notice—its extensive power, and internal constitution,—from the reproofs of their good and sage adviser discovering the ruinous manners and temper of this great corrupted nation;—with pride enough to deprecate shame, and without virtue to avoid it;—often elated without reason, and despondent with as little cause;—magnificent and luxurious in their private, and mean in their public capacity;—at variance for trifles with one another, and passively submitting to every foreign transgression;——bold in their decrees, and dilatory in action;——vainly glorious of the fame of their ancestry, and neglectful of their own;—and envious even of the virtue that served them, as affording too striking a contrast with their own demerits.

CHAP.

CHAP. XI.

SAYS our poet Shakespeare—

————————————O Conspiracy,
Sham'ſt thou to ſhow thy dangerous brow by night,
When evils are moſt free? Oh—then by day
Where wilt thou find a cavern dark enough
To maſk thy monſtrous viſage?—ſeek none—Conſpiracy,
———Hide it in ſmiles and affability!

———So calumny traduces in the voice of candour;—ſo ſeduction pleads in the tone of virtuous love;—ſo the intereſted under the cloak
of friendſhip, ruin the fortunes or peace of the
unwary liſtener to their proteſtations;—ſo every
vice deſtroys under the maſk of ſome virtue—

———Whilſt if it put its native ſemblance on,
Not Erebus itſelf were dim enough
To hide it from prevention!

The miſeries which are entailed upon us by
our love of, and thence our faith in, apparent
virtue,

virtue, belong necessarily (as we are told) to our system, in which good and evil exist but from relation, and in which (as philosophers inculcate) the change of what we suppose bad, might be attended with a privation of what is best :—well!—be it so—as being for the best!——But should experience then tutor us into distrust?—Should we obviate deceit, by tales of fatality incident to good faith, and give up our humanity for the knowledge of mankind?—Or should we go further—trade on the same rules—meet hypocrisy with hypocrisy—and, not satisfied with being adepts, become tricksters at the game of life?——Or lastly, should we give into the reality of every appearance, and implicitly train our judgment to a listless acquiescence in whatever is shown, or told us?—Is there no alternative in this bustling world, but to think for ourselves, and be misanthropes;—or with others, and be dupes?—I hope (as much as many may believe) that the knowledge and love of the world may be easily reconciled;—easy however as it may be, I own myself unequal to the task;—I proceed therefore to the second consideration.

In a private situation, an ignorance of the schemes and machinations employed by men to gratify their appetites, at the expence of their fellow creatures, is assuredly preferable to the most accurate investigation of human morals; a too near acquaintance with which, can serve but to cloud the season of society, and alloy the chearfullness of hospitality with mental reservation: in the narrow circle, deceit may have too little opportunity, or too little effect for the evil consequences thereof to balance the evil consequences of preparing against them,— the loss of internal peace of mind, and of goodwill towards man.

As far then as relates to his own domestic sociality, it is not only allowable, but praiseworthy, for an individual not to embitter his mind by a too nice research into the motives of human words and actions; which, as it convinces him of the depravity of others, is likely to render him too somewhat depraved; or at best to depreciate, with the merits of his associates, the happiness of his life.

As a moral being, he may be permitted (I think) an ignorance of the craftyhood, and wiles around him; but as a being, making part of a state or civil society, he should be well apprized of the snares that lay in wait for him *as such*; his own independant welfare and peace which in the prior case bore the most weight of argument become of little consideration, and he is under indispensable obligation to acquire all such knowledge as may be necessary to the making him a good and servicable citizen; he should be often told, and have much thought, of how many tyrants have gained a first footing on the necks of the people, by bellowing for liberty!——how many have clamoured for freedom, and have overturned the freest of constitutions!—how often patriotism hath been but a name!—he should well have considered what ravages have been committed under the mask of piety; and observe in the annals of mankind, that zealotism is no sign but of madness, protestation no proof of holy fervour, and grimace no part of religion: he should have in view the massacres superstition hath occasioned; and the ravages which ambition hath perpetrated under the cloak of sanctity.

So far the study of mankind is the duty of each member of the state, who for the security,

rity, and many other bleſſings he enjoys under the ſhelter of government, owes his mite towards the obviating every evil which may tend to the ſubverſion or annoyance of the ſocial eſtabliſhment that protects him.

To awaken the attention of the reader to each leſſon recondite in the hiſtory I have undertaken to inveſtigate is the purpoſe of this book; and I hope the various eſſays interwoven with the eventful narrative will not be looked upon as idle, impertinent, or digreſſive; but as appertaining, and even neceſſary to the treatiſe,—— as working out its chief—its *moral* intent.

We are now to have in view a holy war, rendered acceſſary to the ſchemes of ambition; —from zeal and ſuperſtition, made horridly deſtructive to private perſons and property;— from a crafty ſimulation of piety, made ruinous to the rights and liberties of a whole country. The ſucceſs of arms gave to each ſtate with acceſſion of territory, new conſequence and aſcendancy in the common aſſembly of Greece, called the Amphyctionic Council; and that ſuperior intereſt therein (as well may be imagined of a people degenerate from the juſtice and patriot-virtues of their anceſtry) was often employed to

ſelfiſh

selfish ends, to serve the purposes of ambition, or heats of national animosity.

The Thebans from their late course of conquest under Pelopidas and Epaminondas, had acquired a weight sufficient to influence the majority of votes, and in the spirit of revenge they turned the tide of power on their hereditary foes, the Spartans and the Phocians; they managed, on a frivolous pretence, to get a decree past, imposing so heavy a fine, that the respective funds of these states were inadequate to the discharge of it, and thereby they were driven to the odious necessity of warring with the prescriptive supremacy of the great Grecian council: Phocis, from situation, lay readiest for attack, and from national weakness was hopeless of defence; its general Philomelus, conscious of the poor resources, whether of men or of monies that his country could boast, to remedy the evil called in an army of mercenaries; and to have wherewithall to pay and support them, desperately laid hands on the treasures of the Delphic temple, the care and priesthood of which were ever entrusted to the Phocians: the nature of the contest was now changed, and the name of rebellion, hateful

enough

enough in itself, was branded with the epithets of sacrilegious and profane.

Human nature under a similarity of circumstances hath been every where, and in every age the same; the horrors of the sacred war in Greece may be depicted with the like colouring, as the vehement and bloody contests with which the holy madness of zeal, and vanities of heresy have from time to time stained the æra of the most merciful of religions.

The mind deeply employed on what it never can attain, and deeply interested in what it never can be assured of,———recurs for assistance to the universality of opinion, which in proportion to its extent gives comfort and hope to those who unwilling to doubt and unable to believe, rest their security on the belief of others: when any portion of this universality is withdrawn, it must affect each part of the communion, on the totality of which rests the strength of good faith whence each individual mind draws its consolatory peace: in itself, the mind hath found no certitude; in general acquiescence, it hath presumed one; and a privatation of that proof (visionary as it is) of what it hath been taught to wish, and thence to imagine, threatens it with a

state

state of doubt, horror, and despondency, which to avoid, it fancies itself into enthusiasm, or deviates into zealotism and superstition, and at any rate rages against all, who subtracting their authority, have diminished its original resources, and have driven it to frenzy and discontent: this religious fury once awakened, deprives the soul of all happiness but in its madness;——to think, were to dispel that particular prophetic dream of life which habit and hope have made so necessary, and to this the zealot prefers his delirium,——fights blindful, and tilts at all,— who, the bandage from their eyes, are victims to the rage they vainly seek to calm, instead of to oppose.

Religious fury as it is cruel, so is it implacable, whilst it knows not remorse, or mistaking the workings of conscience, blindly seeks peace in the reiterated perpetration of the very crimes that imperceptibly have been the ruin of it.

The very numerous examples of the inveteracy attending religious dissentions, have been, many too recent, and all much too frequent, to render a detail of its spirit of massacre and persecution any longer necessary; and I shall
proceed

proceed to the more public confequences of the Phocian holy war.

The ambitious Philip (as to every other neighbouring ftate) had made pretenfions likewife to Theffaly; but Lycophron ftill fupported a competition with him for the crown, and having acquaintance with the Phocian Onomarchus, he proffered him a reinforcement of Theffalian horfe, provided that he would reciprocally aid him with his mercenaries, if attacked by the Macedonian: the enterprizing activity of Philip foon brought on the expected exigency; and Onomarchus fuccefsfully backed the pretenfions of Lycophron and drove his rival from the field: Philip with a quick eye faw the profit that might be made of this defeat; hitherto the nature of his quarrel with Lycophron had borne the afpect of ufurpation, but his enemy connected with the Phocians was now ftain'd with the odium of their caufe, and might juftly be purfued with all the rancour of piety;—taking the part of the Amphyctions, he was at the fame time conquering his rival, gaining an eftablifhment in Greece, and a fuperior intereft in its determinations and councils; with alacrity therefore he urged the war, forwaded his levies to the field,

field, and attacked the Phocian army, his soldiers hymning the name, and wearing each a laurel sprig in honor, of the Delphic Apollo; Philip gaining an easy victory sent to Thebes to demand the pleasure of that state relative to the treatment of his prisoners, the punishment of whom he left to them as avengers of the profane and sacrilegious depredations on the most holy of Temples: the Thebans flattered by the condescension, and elated with the hopes of alliance with, so powerful a prince, blindly entered into his views by an impolitic solicitation of his further friendship and assistance.

It was at this time that the assembly of Athens was haranguing so haughtily, and acting so remissly with respect to the several enterprizes of Philip: in truth besides the indolent and lascivious temper of the times, much concurred to flatter or to argue the Athenians into an idleness of opposition, that bore, almost the mien of neutrality.

Aristodemus and Neoptolemus sent to pry into the real designs of Philip, received with the most generous affability returned to plead the cause of their benefactor; these men belonged to the theater, but the reader must not suppose,

that

that this their profession any ways affected the authority of their mission, or of their report;—Livy, speaking of the public merits of the actor Aristo, " says—" *nec ars, quia nihil tale apud Græcos pudori eſt, ea deformabat :* two likewiſe of the moſt noble of the citizens, Phrynon and Cteſiphon, viſiting the court of Pella on their own private concerns, came from Macedon with much proof of the munificence, and of courſe with many tales of the juſtice and goodneſs, of the King; and Phocion, at the head of the moſt virtuous and independant party of the ſtate, deem'd it in this degenerate age moſt expedient to temporize, and not expoſe his country to a conteſt which the public corruption and the vices of its conſtituents rendered it moſt inadequate to: when we are told that ſixty of the prime citizens (like Boccacio's mirthful ſeceſſion from the plague of Florence) had totally withdrawn from the aſſemblies, and had formed a ſociety of wit and merriment, the chief rule of which, was, never to think of what concerned the ſtate;—when we are told that ſuch an aſſociation was, was known, and was permitted, we muſt agree with Phocion and the other good and free citizens, that to be ſuch by ſufferance was their

beſt,

best, and indeed only hope: they used the same address to conciliate Philip, as Philip to deceive them; in this very momentous crisis they still had an eye to peace, and when the more spirited or less considerate patriots were bellowing for war, they pleaded for a mediocrity of measures; they reprobated these too great sticklers for old virtues and old manners.—and with reason:—Cicero was right, when he said of Cato—*noces interdùm reipublicæ, dicens, tanquàm in Platonis* Πολιϑειᾳ, *non tanquam in Romuli fæce, sententiam:* this moderate party once again prevailed on the assembly to postpone all hostile preparations, and to depute a more respectable embassy of ten of the principal men of the state to demand a categorical answer from Philip, and to get a clear view into his designs, and into the strength of his kingdom: what is wished, is readily believed; and Philip desirous of not embroiling himself too prematurely with a republic still most populous and wealthy, took advantage of their desires of peace, to deceive the people into a security of it, by the most specious language, and most ingratiating behaviour to their ministers: these ten men were of the best families of Athens, all of much ascendancy, and

all

all of different characters; for the courteous, he had affability; for the proud, honourable attention; money for the avaricious, and liberality to all;—another and another embassy succeeded from which the delegates returned, or deceived themselves, or to deceive their countrymen, and to accuse, and bicker with, one another.

These ministries, during which something like a peace was botched up, served but to give Philip time to proceed on his great design, and to feed the flames of dissention and animosity which long had wasted the strength of Athens: however this compact confined the measures of the republic, it was no bar to the progress of its insidious enemy;—having listened to the solicitations of the Thebans, having joined forces with them on the confines of Phocis, obliged its inhabitants to a discretionary surrender, massacred or enslaved the people, burnt, or dismantled the towns, and having in reward for these services under the Amphyctionic banner, gained a seat in its councils,——he was preparing to turn all these events to account, and on this footing-place to fix the machine that was to shake the universe,—to master Greece, and with Greece to conquer Asia!

Demost-

Demosthenes now once again attempted to awaken his fellow-citizens to an apprehension of the schemes of Philip; and Chares, and afterwards Phocion, were sent at the head of small detachments, to watch over the interests of the republic, and the latter proved some obstacle to the success of the Macedonian arms; but the Locrians now falling under the same imputation, as heretofore the Phocians,——the Greeks, as if rivals for servitude, with the same heat they were emulous of empire, pressed Philip to set forth at the head of the Amphyctionic army, to chastise the delinquents; and thus these exertions of Athens as late, were in vain; for Philip now by invitation, marched into Greece, and and with great show of veneration and piety, accepted the command; whilst favoring oracles, dailily proceeded from the venal tripod, as texts for each traiterous demagogue to discant on, and blind the easy superstitious citizens: too soon, and most fatally they were undeceived, when Philip, at the head of a mighty army, instead of employing it to the religious purpose, for which he had been permitted, without opposition to penetrate thus far, suddenly turned, surprized, fortified, and garrisoned Elatea, a city lying between,

and

and commanding the territories on one side, of Thebes; on the other, of Athens.

Necessity now held the place of virtue; the people were for a moment frightened out of their vices and indolence, and hastily passed a decree that teemed with the spirit of their ancient vigour and constitution; a manifesto was expedited to the chief states of Greece; and a chosen embassy sent to plead their common cause with Thebes; in vain Philip employed every artifice and intrigue to secure the amity of this people; —the allied armies of the Thebans and the Athenians joined to fight for the liberties of the common country.

The battle of Chæronea quickly decided the contest; and Greece,——whose first heroes have been the favorites of poetry,—whose mature and patriotic vigour against the Persian was the ornament of eloquence,——whose struggles in, and convalescence from, intestine commotion, have been the pride of history,—losing its spirit, its freedom, and its policy, was sunk beneath the arms or intrigues of an ambitious king, and left indebted for its every privilege, to his goodwill and sufferance.

C H A P.

CHAP. XII.

A FUNERAL oration in honour of those slain at the battle of Chæronea, was spoken by Demosthenes; the authenticity of the declamation extant, hath been disputed by the scholiast, as not being replete with that sublime eloquence which characterize his other speeches; but surely on such an occasion even a Demosthenes might be allowed to fail; all his views had been frustrated;—every resource of force, or policy exhausted;—Philip, it was not safe to irritate;—the Athenians, it were cruel to depress; and the two sources of invective and sympathy were thus diverted from the particular field of genius, they were the best suited to enrich: every circumstance was delicately to be conducted between the power on one side, and the miseries on the other; and might not too the speaker be supposed embarrassed with so touching, so distressful a subject!——to the declamation of Pericles every Athenian pulse beat full and high;—to repeat

repeat the honors of the dead, brought no shame on the living;—their loss, no ruin on the republic;——and the orator had victory for his theme, and the victorious for his audience! Is no allowance to be made for the difference of the times, or for the feelings of a speaker,———who was to stand up and deliver to a hopeless circle, the funeral oration of their successless friends;—of their liberties;—of their country!

It hath not been unusual to close the history of Greece, at this period; had I undertaken to trace the general history of Greece, I should think myself now approaching to the most interesting part of my work; I should look with a curious eye into the transactions and constitution of the Achæan league; I should busy myself with the Ætolians; I should pry into the various declension of each republic; and build walls to Lacedæmon: even the single state of Athens, I cannot so readily quit, with the simple assertion,—" That the liberties of Greece perished at the field of Cheronæa:"——that they did, should be manifested.

Philip, to sound the temper of the Greeks, and to prepare them for the Asiatic expedition, called a meeting of their delegates to Corinth, and Athens, and every other city (excepting Sparta) obeyed the summons, and in general council coincided with the views of Philip, and acknowledged his title to the command in chief.

Philip lived not to profit of his conquests; his death was deemed favorable to the recovery of liberty and of power; Demosthenes on the news thereof, appeared in the assembly with a chaplet on his head, and exhorted the people to new struggles and opposition; but the bold and vigilant genius of Alexander gave not this spirit time to blaze;—he quickly raised and appeared with a powerful force, and reduced the Athenians to an acquiescence in the terms granted them by his father; and then at the head of his veteran army, went forth, to work out under Providence the great revolution of the East.

The twelve years that Alexander was pursuing his victories in Asia, were a golden period for Greece; a man of a polished and erudite mind could not imagine to himself happier times, —times when flourished philosophy, art, and every requisite to adorn a life of Attic ease:— the visionary might find fellow-dreamers in the groves of Plato;—the subtile might converse with Aristotle;—the grave with Zeno;—the

more

more cheerful moralist might walk the gardens of Epicurus;—and the votary of elegant sensuality might loiter away his noon at the academy of Phidias, and his evening at the table of the witty and luxurious Demades.

It is a curious circumstance that Xerxes, who had yielded to the strength of the republic, from the pillage of the city, carried into Asia with him the statues of Aristogeiton and Harmodius; and that Alexander, who had mastered the republic, sent from Asia, and replaced these very statues of the first assertors of that liberty, he had destroyed. This remark might seem pregnant with little more than conceit, did it not not lead to an observation on the ill-policy of Alexander, who, surely was little considerate of the peace and security of his government, when he sent to Athens this inflammatory present, —being ever before their eyes a memorial of their past honors, and present ignominy;—ever reproaching them with their abject acquiescence in a servitude, shameful, however light, and ever with this passive temper strongly contrasting the spirit of their ancient martyrs to freedom.

The conqueror's ill-timed generosity may be presumed, I think, to have had some such effect;

fect; for in the last book of Arrian, remarking a general embassy of the Greeks addressing Alexander as a deity, at the same time I remember an exception (mentioned in the twelfth chapter of the fifth book of Ælian) with respect to the Athenians, who roused from their servile complacency, fined the orator Demades for a mere proposal of his apotheosis; and when the heroic king sent his mandate to Greece, ordering each city to receive back its exiles, we find Athens then too (and almost singly) opposing the conqueror's good will and pleasure; and Alexander a little before his death, had collected a mighty force,—(says Justin) *ad delendas Athenas*;—but he was cut off in his career of victory; and the Athenians had time to make warlike preparations, wherewith to dispute the sovereignty of his successors.

The vast empire of Alexander, hereditary and acquired, being divided amongst his captains; Macedon, and Greece as its appendant, fell to the share of Antipater; who immediately proceeded to chastise his refractory subjects of Ætolia and Athens: Leosthenes chosen general of the united forces of the states, gained a signal victory over the new usurper, and drove him to
a re-

a refuge, and closely besieged him, in the city of Lamia: this last struggle of the Athenians was for a time bravely supported; though Leosthenes had fallen in a skirmish before the gates, yet his army was not dispirited, but still closely invested the place, and in a set engagement of the cavalry of the two powers again carried off the palm of victory: Antipater no longer thinking himself safe within the town, secretly withdrew;—— but soon again was heard of at the head of the formidable fleets of Macedon; the Athenians vigorously then prepared to beat him too from the seas, and quickly they had a fleet of an hundred and seventy sail boldly in quest of their enemy.

Looking back a few years to the inactive and remiss conduct of this people towards Philip, I could not with-hold my astonishment at the sudden change from dissention and supine weakness, to this present spirit of unanimous and vigorous exertion; to account for the vicissitude, I must attribute it to the effects of the times, when Alexander roved from kingdom to kingdom, through Asia, and left Greece to enjoy (what I should call)—— *the liberal Age:* in the various schools, politics were reduced to a science, and morals to a system; philosophy

gave

gave strength, and the polite arts gave ease, and the general activity of the mind gave to it vigour and spirit; the theory of what men ought to do was becoming diffusive, and from its novelties, not yet tedious; and it had attained refinement enough to attach, and had simplicity enough not to elude, the attention: the Athenians proud of the distinctions which accrued to them from the Portico and the Academe, gave readily and generally into the amusements and studies that ennobled their hour of peace, and from these studies, the citizens may be supposed to have acquired something like, what in modern language is called, *'Point of Honour*;——a sentiment which internally forbids a too easy cession of any pretension made whether to justice, to valour, to wisdom, to virtue, or (in a word) to any rare and admired quality:——The Athenians curiously investigating the duties of a man, and of a citizen, in some degree the practice thereof ensued,—talking and writing of the spirit of their republican constitution, they seemed the more bound to its support;——a fortunate success on the first outset encouraged the people to go on, and had they finally been victorious in the contest, perhaps Montesquieu had been obliged to wave his ingenious syſtem, and acknowledge the exiſtence of a free and well conſtituted democracy, whoſe principle was—*Honour.*

Perdiccas reinforcing the fleets of Antipater, they overpowered and deſtroyed the whole Athenian armament, and appearing triumphant before Athens, compelled the citizens to a diſcretionary ſurrender, and making ſome change in the commonwealth, left Demetrius governor over it, at the head of a numerous garriſon: Antipater on his entrance into Athens immediately baniſhed twenty two thouſand from the city; Theſe, ſays Diodorus, were only thoſe who had not the cenſus neceſſary to the conſtituting a citizen according to the new regulations; but we may be certain, I think, that Antipater loſt not the opportunity of ſecuring his government by baniſhing all, whoſe great and leading qualities might gain the aſcendant over his innovations;——it is probable that the old intimacy of virtue and poverty was not broken,——that the good and indigent went together into exile,—and that to be abjeƈt, as well as to be wealthy, was ſome title to favour; we may therefore pronounce it glorious (and it was the laſt glory of this republic)—on ſuch an occaſion to have loſt *ſo many* citizens.

It may be asked———" did not Demetrius Poliorcetes sometime afterwards drive the Phalerean from his government, and restore liberty to Athens?"———Liberty, I answer, it was then incapable of receiving: for the truth of this, recur to the lives of Plutarch,———behold this refuse of the citizens, with a servility that disclaims the name of gratitude, enrolling this deliverer with their gods,———decreeing him the honors of Ceres and Bacchus,———making an oracle of him,———carrying their devotion to so fulsome a pitch, that Demetrius himself, at length, deeming them unworthy of further tenderness or management, taxed them at once two hundred and fifty talents, and in the very presence of the ministers who brought it, threw it into the lap of his harlot Lamia.

It was mightily the fashion of Alexander's captains, to be very bountiful———*of liberty to Greece*;———Telesphorus came with it from Antigonus, and Polyperchon sent it from the Peloponnese;———but to close my book, and obviate further objection with the authority of Livy———[*civitas*]—*ea autem in libertate est posita, quæ suis stat viribus, non ex alieno arbitrio pendet.*

F I N I S.

www.ingramcontent.com/pod-product-compliance
Lightning Source LLC
Chambersburg PA
CBHW022050230426
43672CB00008B/1123